SURVIVAL ENGLISH

English Through Conversations

Book 3

SECOND EDITION

Lee Mosteller

Bobbi Paul
San Diego Community Colleges

Illustrated by Jesse Gonzales

PRENTICE HALL REGENTS, Englewood Cliffs, New Jersey 07632

Acquisitions editor: Nancy Leonhardt
Director of Production and Manufacturing: David Riccardi
Editorial production/design manager: Dominick Mosco
Electronic/production supervision, interior design,
    page composition, and realia design: Paula D. Williams
Electronic Art: Rolando Corujo and Todd Ware
Cover Design Coordinator: Merle Krumper
Production Coordinator: Ray Keating

Illustrations by: Jesse Gonzalez

© 1995 by PRENTICE HALL REGENTS
Prentice-Hall, Inc.
A Simon & Schuster Company
Englewood Cliffs, New Jersey 07632

Printed in the United States of America

10 9 8 7 6 5 4 3 2

ISBN 0-13-878166-4

Prentice-Hall International (UK) Limited, *London*
Prentice-Hall of Australia Pty. Limited, *Sydney*
Prentice-Hall Canada Inc., *Toronto*
Prentice-Hall Hispanoamericana, S. A., *Mexico*
Prentice-Hall of India Private Limited, *New Delhi*
Prentice-Hall of Japan, Inc., *Tokyo*
Simon & Schuster Asia Pte. Ltd., *Singapore*
Editora Prentice-Hall do Brasil, Ltda., *Rio de Janeiro*

Preface

··

This workbook has been designed by teachers of begnning ESL students. It is written for students who have limited oral vocabulary, a slightly better reading ability and good use of the alphabet. These students will have had one or two semesters of ESL, but are still considered, beginners. *Survival English: English Through Conversations, Book 1* and *Survival English: English Through Conversations, Book 2* are good prerequisites for this book. Students at this level bring common experiences from the community to the classroom as well as a motivation to learn the survival skills necessary to function in daily life.

This book is organized to develop and practice listening, speaking, reading, and writing skills, in common situations. There is, however, a greater emphasis on writing in this book than in the previous two books in the series. The competency-based dialogues are the core of the book. The dialogues provide listening and speaking practice incorporated with familiar and necessary living skills. They are followed by charts, reading and writing passages, sequence stories, and exercises to reinforce and practice the competencies introduced in the dialogues. They are divided into nine content areas, each appropriate for the low-literate adult learner.

Contents

3 HEALTH

DIALOGUES

SAFETY

4 DIALOGUES

THE SURVIVAL ENGLISH SERIES

By Lee Mosteller and Bobbi Paul

      Book 1
      Book 1A: chapters 1–5 of Book 1
      Book 1B: chapters 6–10 of Book 1
      Instructor's Manual for Book 1

By Lee Mosteller and Michele Haight:

      Book 2
      Book 2A: chapters 1–4 of Book 2
      Book 2B: chapters 5–9 of Book 2
      Instructor's Manual for Book 2

By Lee Mosteller and Bobbi Paul

      Book 3
      Book 3A: chapters 1–4 of Book 3
      Book 3B: chapters 5–9 of Book 3
      Instructor's Manual for Book 3

SURVIVAL ENGLISH

1

SCHOOL

A. Welcome back to school. It's nice to see you again.

B. Thank you.

A. How was your | vacation?
 weekend?
 holiday? |

B. It was | great.
 O.K.
 not so good. |

A. Did you | practice <br> use <br> write <br> speak | any English?

B. Yes, I did. I practiced a little bit of English.

· ·

Yes, I did. I | used <br> read <br> wrote <br> spoke | a lot of English.

No, I didn't. I didn't | practice <br> use <br> read <br> write <br> speak | any English.

Practice using the same answers.

Yes,	I he she we they	did.

1. Did you use any English? _____.

2. Did he practice any English? _____.

3. Did she read any English? _____.

4. Did they write any English? _____.

5. Did your family speak any English? _____.

6. Did Ly practice any English? _____.

7. Did Jorge use any English? _____.

Practice using these short answers.

No,	I he she we they	didn't.

8. Did you read any English? _____.

9. Did May practice any English? _____.

10. Did Nilofar write any English? _____.

11. Did Ann use any English? _____.

12. Did Liem and Tuyen speak any English? _____.

13. Did your family practice any English? _____.

14. Did he use any English? _____.

Practice using some longer answers.

Yes,	I he she we they	spoke practiced read wrote used	some English.

1. Did you use any English?

_____.

2. Did he practice any English?

_____.

3. Did she read any English?

_____.

4. Did they write any English?

_____.

Practice using some longer answers.

No,	I he she we they	didn't	speak practice read write use	any English.

5. Did Tom and Sue speak any English?

_____.

6. Did he practice any English?

_____.

7. Did your family use any English?

_____.

8. Did Ann use any English?

_____.

SCHOOL 2

A. What school do you go to?

B. _____.

A. Where is it?

B. It's in _____ on _____.
　　　　　　　(city)　　　　　　　(street)

A. What are you studying?

B. _____.

A. Who's your teacher?

B. _____.

A. How much does it cost?

B. Nothing, it's free.

1. Fill out this card or make a copy to fill out.
2. Give copies to your children, friends, and family.
3. Tell them to put the card in their wallets.
4. In case of an emergency, they can call you at school.

Child's Name:	_____
Parent's Name:	_____
	_____
Parent's School:	_____
Days:	_____
Time: From _____	To _____
Parent's School Telephone:	_____
Parent's Teacher's Name:	_____

A. Good morning. I'm _____.

I want to $\boxed{\begin{array}{l}\text{come to}\\\text{enroll in}\\\text{study in}\end{array}}$ an English class.

B. Did you study here before?

A. No, I didn't. I went to another school.

B. That's fine. Where are you from?

A. I was born in _____, but I have lived here for _____.

B. I'll get you a registration card.

```
┌──────────────────────────────────────────────────────────┐
│                  REGISTRATION FORM                         │
│                     PLEASE PRINT                           │
│  STUDENT'S NAME  Garcia                Erik                │
│                   (LAST NAME)           (FIRST NAME)       │
│  SOCIAL SECURITY NUMBER          DATE OF BIRTH      SEX    │
│  6 2 9 - 4 0 - 5 1 3 7 | 0 4 - 2 7 - 6 9 | ☑M ☐F          │
│  ADDRESS    4373          North Ave.  #81                  │
│             (NUMBER)          (STREET)                     │
│  Houston      TX          77009       713_555_6829         │
│  (CITY)       (STATE)     (ZIP CODE)  AREA CODE  PHONE NUMBER│
│  COUNTRY OF ORIGIN  Costa Rica                             │
│  LOCAL EMERGENCY CONTACT _____               │
│                           (LAST NAME)    (FIRST NAME)      │
│  LOCAL EMERGENCY NUMBER _____                │
│                                                            │
│  STUDENT'S SIGNATURE  Erik Garcia                          │
│  TODAY'S DATE   6-16-94                                     │
│  INSTRUCTOR'S SIGNATURE  Bobbi Paul                        │
│  DATE ENTERED CLASS  6-16-94                                │
└──────────────────────────────────────────────────────────┘
```

REGISTRATION FORM
PLEASE PRINT

STUDENT'S NAME ___Garcia_____Erik_____
                    (LAST NAME)   (FIRST NAME)

SOCIAL SECURITY NUMBER   DATE OF BIRTH   SEX
6 2 9 - 4 0 - 5 1 3 7 | 0 4 - 2 7 - 6 9 | ☑M ☐F

ADDRESS ___4373_____North Ave. #81_____
            (NUMBER)   (STREET)

Houston_____TX_____77009_____713 - 555 - 6829
(CITY)   (STATE)   (ZIP CODE)   AREA CODE   PHONE NUMBER

COUNTRY OF ORIGIN _Costa Rica_____

LOCAL EMERGENCY CONTACT _____
                         (LAST NAME)   (FIRST NAME)

LOCAL EMERGENCY NUMBER _____

STUDENT'S SIGNATURE __Erik Garcia_____

TODAYS DATE ___6-16-94_____

INSTRUCTOR'S SIGNATURE ___Bahli Paul_____

DATE ENTERED CLASS ___6-16-94_____

1. Look at the registration card.   Check YES or NO.

2. Is the last name Smith?   Yes ___ No ___

3. Is the first name Jones?   Yes ___ No ___

4. Is the person a woman?   Yes ___ No ___

5. Did he fill in the telephone number? Yes ___ No ___

6. Did he fill in his social security   Yes ___ No ___
number?

7. Did he sign his registration card?   Yes ___ No ___

8. Did the teacher sign the   Yes ___ No ___
registration card?

9. Did he write an emergency number?   Yes ___ No ___

10. Is the student from Eretria?   Yes ___ No ___

11. Did you read questions 1–11?   Yes ___ No ___

School Supplies

1.

2.

3.

4.

5.

6.

7.

8.

9.

10.

11.

12.

13.

14.

15.

Make a question.

		tape?
		computer?
		stapler?
Do you have		dictionary?
Who has		hole punch?
Where is	a the	typewriter?
Do you need		ruler?
Is there		copy machine
		tape recorder?
		calculator?
		white out?

		notebooks?
Do you have		paper clips?
Who has		thumbtacks?
Where are	the	staples?
Do you need		text books?
		rubber bands?

A. Excuse me, what time do we take a break?

B. We take a break at 10:30.

A. Thanks. Where are the restrooms?

B. Go outside. They're on the right.
They're next to our room.

A. Thanks again.

Where	is are	the	pencil sharpener? coffee? bookstore? library? books? restrooms?

BOOKSTORE
OPEN
MONDAY - FRIDAY
8 AM - 8 PM

1.

2.

3.

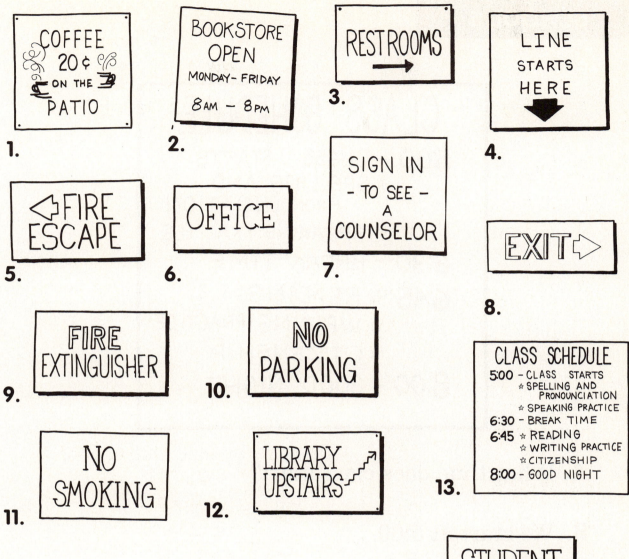

1. COFFEE 20¢ ON THE PATIO

2. BOOKSTORE OPEN MONDAY - FRIDAY 8 AM — 8 PM

3. RESTROOMS →

4. LINE STARTS HERE ↓

5. ← FIRE ESCAPE

6. OFFICE

7. SIGN IN - TO SEE - A COUNSELOR

8. EXIT →

9. FIRE EXTINGUISHER

10. NO PARKING

11. NO SMOKING

12. LIBRARY UPSTAIRS

13. CLASS SCHEDULE
5:00 - CLASS STARTS
☆ SPELLING AND PRONOUNCIATION
☆ SPEAKING PRACTICE
6:30 - BREAK TIME
6:45 ☆ READING
☆ WRITING PRACTICE
☆ CITIZENSHIP
8:00 - GOOD NIGHT

14.  STUDENT PARKING

A. Can we smoke here?

B. Where do we go in case of fire?

C. Are there bathrooms?

D. Is there an office?

E. How much is the coffee?

F. Where can I park?

G. When can we buy a book?

H. Where is the library?

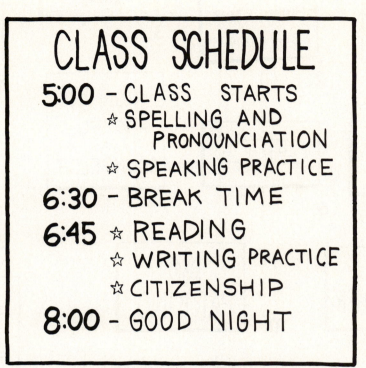

A. What time does class start?

B. We start at 5:00.

A. What time does it finish?

B. We finish at 8:00, but we take a 15 minute break at 6:30.

A. A break?

B. Yes, we walk around, use the restroom, have a cup of coffee, and visit with other students.

SCHOOL 6

A. Why do you come to school?

B. I want to | read
write
speak | more English.

A. What do you need your English for?

B. I want to _____.

Check what you want to do.

1. I want to read my bills. ____
         the newspapers. ____
         advertisements. ____
         work manuals. ____
         the TV Guide. ____
         the *U.S.Constitution*. ____

2. I want to write letters. ____
         notes. ____
         forms for work. ____
         my story. ____
         love letters. ____

3. I want to speak with neighbors. ____
         sales clerks. ____
         teachers. ____
         doctors. ____
         repairmen. ____
         landlords. ____
         job supervisors. ____

Raul's Future

Raul Vega lives in the United States. He used to live in Mexico City, Mexico. Raul works in a donut shop. He gets up early and works before school. Then at 8:00 he goes to class, and after class he works again. He mixes the donut batter now, but one day he wants to manage the shop.

Raul speaks Spanish at home and with his friends. But he has to speak English with his boss, the manager. He needs to learn more English to speak with the manager and customers. He needs to read and write in English so he can become a manager.

Here are five words from the story. Underline them in the story. Use them in a new sentence.

1. before _____

2. after _____

3. manager _____

4. early _____

5. customers _____

Reread the story about Raul Vega on page 14.
Write the answers.

1. Who mixes the donut batter?

_____

2. When does Raul go to school?

_____

3. When does Raul work?

_____

4. Where is he from?

_____

5. Where does he work?

_____

6. What language does he speak at home?

_____

7. What language does he speak to his manager?

_____

8. Why does he need to speak more English?

_____

9. Why does he need to read and write English?

_____

10. When do you go to school?

_____

11. What language do you speak at home?

_____

12. Why do you need to speak more English?

_____

Write about yourself.

1. My name is _____.

2. I speak _____.

3. I'm from _____.

4. I have lived here _____.

5. I go to _____ School.

6. I have gone to school for _____.

7. I speak _____ at home.

8. I need to speak English to _____.

9. I need to read and write English to _____.

Interview a friend in the classroom.

10. My friend's name is _____.

11. He / She speaks _____.

12. He / She is from _____.

13. He / She has lived here _____.

14. He / She has gone to school for _____.

15. He / She needs to speak English to _____.

16. He / She needs to read and write English to _____

_____.

A. Did you have a good week at school?

B. Yes, I did.

A. What did you learn?

B. _____

A. What did you enjoy studying?

B. _____

A. What part of school do you like the most?

B. _____

A. What do you like the least?

B. _____

Talk about it.

1. Are schools different in your native country?

2. How are they the same?

3. How are they different?

2

FAMILY AND SOCIAL LIFE

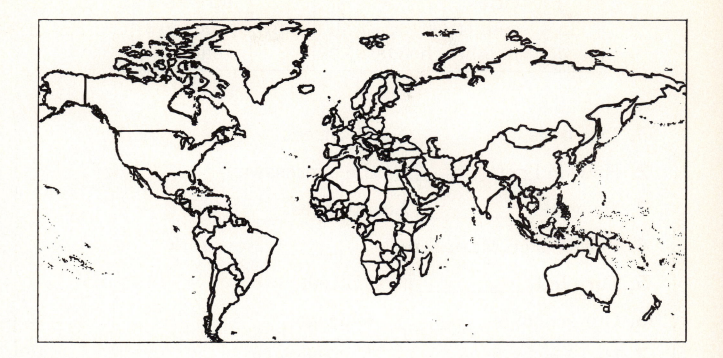

A. Who do you live with?

B. I live | by myself.
| alone.
| with my _____.

How about you?

A. I live with my friend.

B. Where is your family?

A. They're in Switzerland now.

Complete the sentences using **in** or **on**.

in	cities countries neighborhoods		on	streets freeways roads

1. Tom lives _____ North Street.

2. How do I get _____ the expressway?

3. He works _____ Los Angeles.

4. Pat lives on Main Street _____ New York.

5. Turn left _____ First Street.

6. Our school is _____ Chicago.

7. He likes to drive _____ freeways.

8. The casinos are _____ the Strip _____ Las Vegas.

9. The library is _____ the corner.

10. There are millions of people _____ China.

11. Drive carefully _____ streets near schools.

12. They're living _____ Miami now.

13. They used to live _____ San Jose.

14. The hospital is _____ Lincoln Avenue.

15. My friend lives _____ El Paso now.

16. I want to see the pyramids _____ Mexico.

17. You need to get _____ Interstate 5.

18. We thought they lived _____ San Diego.

19. The president lives _____ Washington, D.C.

20. There are many cars _____ the roads now.

Looks and Personalities

Looks are easy to describe. We can see if someone is tall or short.

Personality is more difficult to describe. A personality describes how a person seems to others.

The words below describe personality or looks. Write them in the correct column.

easy going	friendly	serious	forgetful
heavy	old	short	attractive
happy-go-lucky	tall	kind	thin
intelligent	shy	young	outgoing

looks

1. _____
2. _____
3. _____
4. _____
5. _____
6. _____
7. _____

personality

1. _____
2. _____
3. _____
4. _____
5. _____
6. _____
7. _____
8. _____
9. _____

Describe yourself.

_____

_____

_____

Describe the person sitting next to you.

_____

_____

_____

Describe your teacher.

_____

_____

_____

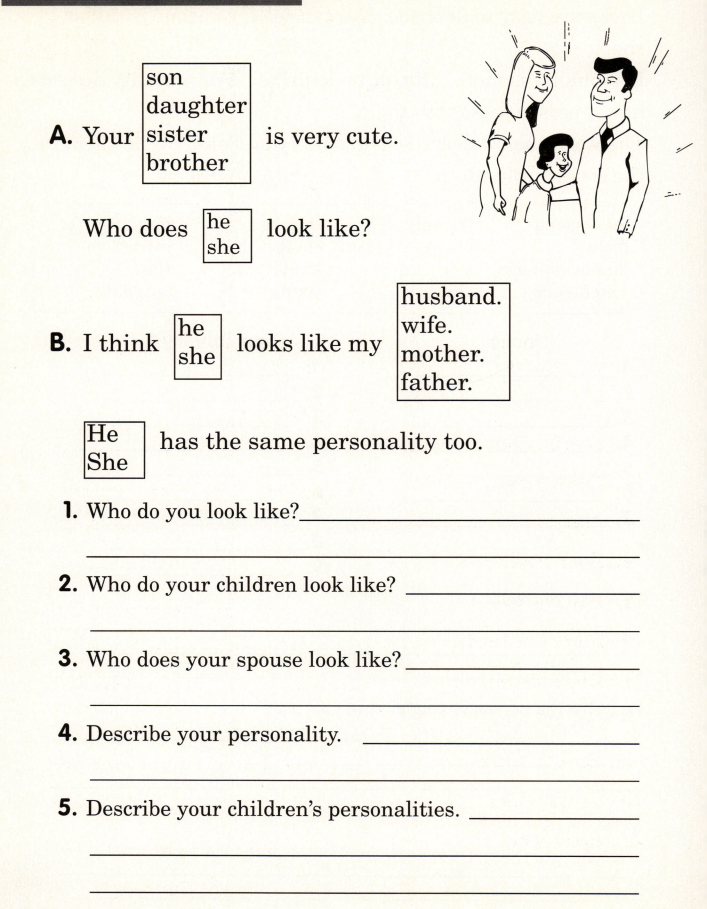

A. Your
| son |
| daughter |
| sister |
| brother |
is very cute.

Who does
| he |
| she |
look like?

B. I think
| he |
| she |
looks like my
| husband. |
| wife. |
| mother. |
| father. |

| He |
| She |
has the same personality too.

1. Who do you look like?_____

_____

2. Who do your children look like? _____

_____

3. Who does your spouse look like? _____

_____

4. Describe your personality. _____

_____

5. Describe your children's personalities. _____

_____

_____

Who is Who?

1. Tom's parents are _____.

2. Peter's grandmother is _____.

3. Mary's husband is _____.

4. Bob's nephew is _____.

5. Sallie's aunt is _____.

6. Mary's sister-in-law is _____.

7. Bob's sister-in-law is _____.

8. Henry's grandson is _____.

9. Peter's uncles are _____.

10. Tom's wife is _____.

11. Bob's niece is _____.

My Family

1. _____ is the oldest in my family.

2. _____ is the youngest in my family.

3. _____ is the prettiest in my family.

4. _____ is the smartest in my family.

5. _____ is the nicest in my family.

6. _____ is the happiest in my family.

7. _____ is the tallest in my family.

8. _____ is the shortest in my family.

9. _____ is the healthiest in my family.

10. _____ is the quietest in my family.

11. _____ speaks the most English in my family.

My Family

1. My family is
large.
small.
nice.
friendly.
happy.

2. I am
single.
engaged.
married.
separated.
divorced.
widowed.
remarried.

3. I have
no children.
one child.
two children.
two sons.
three daughters.
five kids.
two stepchildren.
eight grandchildren.

Write three true sentences about yourself.

_____

_____

_____

Write three true sentences about a classmate.

_____

_____

_____

My Family

1. I'm taller than _____ in my family.

2. _____ is taller than I am.

3. I'm older than _____.

4. _____ is older than I am.

5. I am younger than _____.

6. _____ is younger than I am.

7. I am more outgoing than _____.

8. _____ is more outgoing than I am.

9. _____ has more children than _____.

10. _____ has more children than I do.

11. I am quieter than _____.

12. _____ is quieter than I am.

13. I speak more English than _____.

14. _____ speaks more English than I do.

In or On?

in	a season a month a time a place	on	a date a day a street

1. I met my husband _____ school.

2. We got married _____ the spring.

3. We got married _____ June 1, 1983.

4. _____ July we had our first argument.

5. I thought we were _____ trouble.

6. Then _____ the afternoon he said, "Sorry."

7. _____ five years we had three children.

8. The first child was born _____ May 12, 1984.

9. The second child was born _____ April 1985.

10. The third child was born _____ San Diego _____ July 10, 1987.

11. The three children are _____ school now.

12. They play _____ a soccer team.

13. Now we're living _____ Kennedy Avenue _____ Denver.

14. We're busy and never _____ time. We're always late.

15. Every day _____ the evening, we visit together.

16. Sometimes we go _____ a walk _____ the park.

17. Sometimes we sit _____ a restaurant and talk.

Shekwa's Story

I grew up in Afghanistan. When I was 16 years old I was engaged, but I had never met my future husband. The marriage was arranged by our parents. My husband was in India. He was a medical student. After he finished school in India he became a doctor there. Then he came back to Afghanistan and we were married. Before that we only saw pictures of each other. I was almost 18 years old when I was married.

Now we are a small family. I have one daughter and one son. My daughter is seven months old and my son is two years old.

We are a happy family. We have a good life.

1. Where did Shekwa grow up? _____

2. How did she meet her husband?

_____

_____

3. How old was she when she was engaged?

_____

4. She got married when she was _____ years old.

5. Her husband is in the _____ profession.

6. Where were you when you got married?_____

7. How did you meet your husband or wife? _____

_____

8. How old were you when you got married? _____

MAIN CINEMA

It's a Wonderful Day (G)
1:30   4:00   6:30   9:00
Mountain Valley 555-1888

A. What time does the movie start?

B. _____.

A. What time is it over?

B. _____. What rating does it have?

A. It's rated G.

Movie Ratings

G   – general

PG – parental guidance

PG – must be 13 or be with parent

R   – restricted

X   – adult

NR – not rated

Movies

1. Do you go to movie theaters or do you watch videos?

_____

2. What was the last video or movie that you saw?

_____

3. What kind of movies or videos do you like?

_____

4. What's your favorite movie?

_____

5. Who is your favorite actor or actress?

_____

6. Do you know what G, PG, PG13, R, and X stand for?

Write the correct abbreviation next to the words.

_____ parental guidance—not for kids under 13

_____ parental guidance for all children

_____ general—no sex, no violence; OK for family

_____ restricted—17 and over

_____ X-rated—over 21; sex and violence

Theater Snack Bar

SNACK BAR

Coffee	1.00
Coke sm.	1.50
lg.	2.00
Popcorn sm.	2.00
lg.	3.00
Candy lg.	1.50
Ice-cream	1.75
Hot-dogs	2.25

1. How much are two small cokes and a cup of coffee? _____

2. Buy two small cokes and a cup of coffee. Give them $5.00. How much change will you get? _____

3. Buy 1 small popcorn and two large candy bars. Give them $5.00. How much change will you get? _____

4. Buy two hot dogs and two large cokes for you and your friend. How much do they cost together? _____

5. How much more is the ice cream than a small coke? _____

6. Do three ice creams cost more than two large cokes?   Yes   No

7. Do a coffee and an ice cream cost less than two small cokes?   Yes   No

8. Is a hot dog cheaper than an ice cream?   Yes   No

9. Do you have enough money in your pocket for one of everything?   Yes   No

10. Can you buy me a cup of coffee?   Yes   No

Jose's Date

Jose is a single, good-looking man. He likes to go out with beautiful women. He always has discount movie tickets that he buys at work.

Tonight he is having dinner at Maria's house. About 7:30 they decide to see a movie. They want to see *The Chase*. They look in the newspaper, but the movie started at 7:00.

What can they do instead of going to a movie?

They can

play checkers
go for a ride
watch TV
go get ice cream
visit friends
rent videos
take a walk
listen to music

instead.

1. Where do you think Maria and Jose decide to go?

_____

2. What time did the movie start? _____

3. What time is it now? _____

4. Where does Jose buy his movie tickets? _____

5. How old is Jose? _____

6. How old is Maria? _____

Talk about it.

1. How old are people when they date in your native country?

2. Who pays for the date?

3. Can a single man and a single woman go out together?

4. Where do you like to go on a date?

Talk to five people in your class. Put their names in the left column. Ask questions from the chart and record their answers (yes or no) for each question.

	Do you like to...			
Name	eat out on Sunday nights?	visit friends?	listen to music?	watch TV?
1.				
2.				
3.				
4.				
5.				

Use the chart to answer these questions.

1. Who likes to eat out?_____

2. Who likes to visit friends? _____

3. Who likes to listen to music?_____

4. Who likes to watch T.V.? _____

5. Who doesn't like to watch T.V.? _____

6. Who doesn't like to listen to music?_____

7. Who doesn't like to visit friends?_____

8. Who doesn't like to eat out?_____

A. I've worked a lot lately.

B. Do you have a day off?

A. Yes, I have tomorrow off.

B. What plans do you have?

A. I think I'll | go to a movie.
visit with friends.
go dancing.
go to the beach.
go to the park.
play with my children.
go to church.
look at cars.
go camping.
play with my grandchildren.
go to the mall.

1. What plans do you have for the weekend?

_____

_____

2. What plans do you have for your day off?

_____

_____

3. What plans do your classmates have? Ask three of them.

_____

_____

_____

Talk about it.

In your native country what do people do on their days off?

A. Let's go to the new mall.

B. Great. I saw an ad for cassettes. Do you know where the record store is?

A. No, I don't. But when we get there we can check it.

Mall Directory

Clothing	**level 1**
Electronics	**level 2**
Speciality Shops	**level 2**
Food Court	**level 3**
Theaters	**level 3**

---

1. On what level would you find shoes for your son? _____

2. On what level would you find a movie? _____

3. On what level would you find a birthday card? _____

4. On what level would you find a hamburger? _____

5. On what level would you find a man's shirt? _____

6. On what level would you find a record store? _____

7. On what level would you find a Mexican restaurant? _____

The Mall Directory

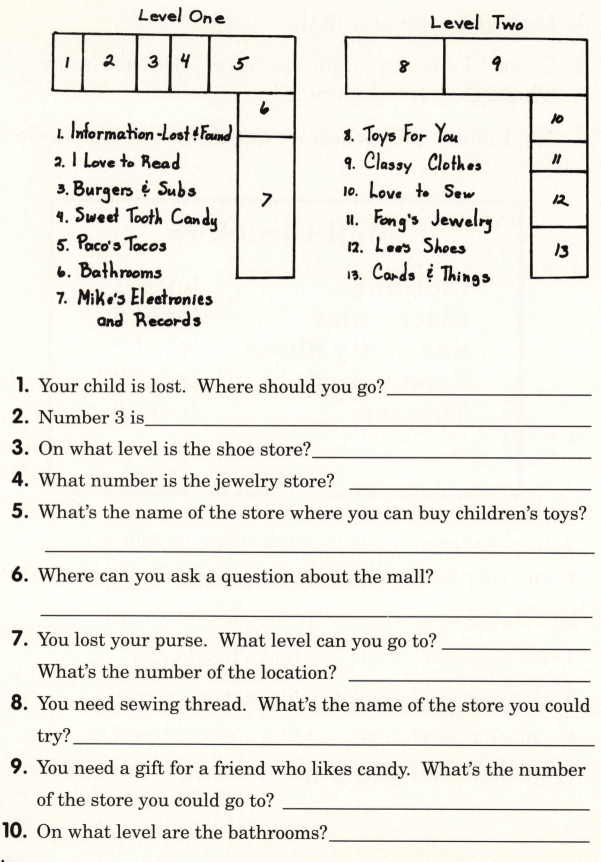

Level One

1	2	3	4	5

6

7

1. Information - Lost & Found
2. I Love to Read
3. Burgers & Subs
4. Sweet Tooth Candy
5. Paco's Tacos
6. Bathrooms
7. Mike's Electronics and Records

Level Two

8	9

10

11

12

13

8. Toys For You
9. Classy Clothes
10. Love to Sew
11. Fong's Jewelry
12. Lee's Shoes
13. Cards & Things

1. Your child is lost. Where should you go? _____

2. Number 3 is _____

3. On what level is the shoe store? _____

4. What number is the jewelry store? _____

5. What's the name of the store where you can buy children's toys?
   _____

6. Where can you ask a question about the mall?
   _____

7. You lost your purse. What level can you go to? _____
   What's the number of the location? _____

8. You need sewing thread. What's the name of the store you could
   try? _____

9. You need a gift for a friend who likes candy. What's the number
   of the store you could go to? _____

10. On what level are the bathrooms? _____

A. I'm going to a party. Would you like to come?

B. Yes, I would. What can I bring?

A. Don't bring anything. Just come.

B. Maybe I'll bring some
| potato chips. |
| drinks. |
| crackers. |
| cheese. |
| wine. |
| beer. |
| _____ |
| _____ |

A. That would be fine.

Invite your friend
to your party.

Help color this party
exciting and bright,
With you at the party
it's a special night!

For _____

Date _____

Time _____

Place _____

_____

Pat's Story

Pat lives alone in a big city. He's new in the United States. He doesn't have any friends yet. He would like to make friends and meet new people, but he doesn't know how. How is he feeling? What's the problem? What can he do?

What do you think?

1. Describe Pat's feelings _____

_____

_____

2. Why does he feel that way? _____

_____

_____

3. What can he do about his problem?_____

_____

_____

Talk about it.

Who was your first friend in this country?
How did you meet your friend?

3

HEALTH

A. Are your daughter's shots up-to-date?

B. I think so. Here's her immunization record.

A. It looks up to date. Does she take any drugs?

B. Drugs?

A. Medication.

B. Medication? Do you mean medicine?

A. Yes, prescription medicine.

B. No, she doesn't.

Talk about it. Then write about it.

1. Does anyone in your family take medication?

_____

2. Who takes medicine in your family?

_____

3. What medications do they take?

_____

4. Why do they take them?

_____

Immunizations

| IMMUNIZATION CARD | VACCINE | DATE GIVEN | DOCTOR OFFICE OR CLINIC |

IMMUNIZATION CARD

NAME. _____

BIRTHDATE _____

ALLERGIES. _____

VACCINE REACTIONS _____

RETAIN THIS DOCUMENT

VACCINE	DATE GIVEN	DOCTOR OFFICE OR CLINIC
Polio	5/74	
Polio	7/74	
DTP/Td	10/75	
MMR	7/76	

There are two kinds of medicine. One medicine prevents you from getting sick. The other medicine helps you get better when you are sick. The medicine that prevents you from getting sick is called an immunization. A doctor or nurse fills in the immunization record for you.

Children must have their immunizations before they go to school. You have to take your child's immunization record when you register him or her for school. The school checks the record to be sure the child's shots are up to date.

Adults need immunizations sometimes. Adults should check with their doctor. You can get your immunizations at the health department, at a health clinic, or at your doctor's office.

Circle the best answer.

1. An immunization
   a. keeps you from getting sick.
   b. helps you get better when you are sick.

2. Children need to have immunizations
   a. several different times on schedule.
   b. only once in their lifetime.

3. Children need to have their immunizations
   a. any time.
   b. before they can go to school.

4. You take your child's immunization record
   a. when you register him or her for school.
   b. after school begins.

5. You can get immunizations at
   a. the health department, health clinic, or your doctor's office.
   b. school, the library, or the post office.

6. Adults
   a. don't need immunizations.
   b. need immunizations occasionally.

A. Have you had a flu shot?

B. No, I haven't. Do you think it's a good idea?

A. Yes, I do. I get a flu shot every year.

B. Are there any side effects?

A. Sometimes. You should ask your doctor.

B. Maybe I will. The flu is terrible.

Cold Symptoms	**Flu Symptoms**
chills	cough
stuffy nose	stuffy nose
headache	headache
fever	fever
tiredness	nausea or vomiting
	diarrhea

In The Emergency Room

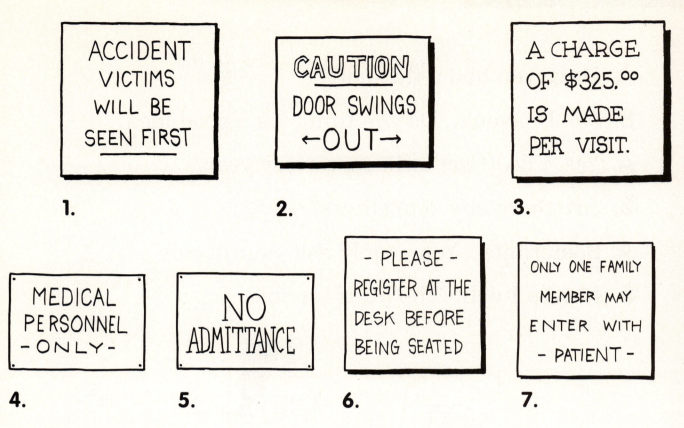

1. ACCIDENT VICTIMS WILL BE SEEN FIRST

2. CAUTION DOOR SWINGS ←OUT→

3. A CHARGE OF $325.⁰⁰ IS MADE PER VISIT.

4. MEDICAL PERSONNEL -ONLY-

5. NO ADMITTANCE

6. - PLEASE - REGISTER AT THE DESK BEFORE BEING SEATED

7. ONLY ONE FAMILY MEMBER MAY ENTER WITH - PATIENT -

Matching

_____ **A.** Be careful, the door opens out.

_____ **B.** It's $325 to see a doctor.

_____ **C.** People hurt in accidents go first.

_____ **D.** One person can go in with the patient.

_____ **E.** Only doctors and nurses can come in here.

_____ **F.** You cannot go in.

_____ **G.** Sign in first.

In The Emergency Room

A. Can I help you?

B. I think my son broke his arm.

A. What's the last name?

B. Washington.

A. The screening nurse will call you. Wait over there.

Check the reasons you would go to the emergency room.

_____ **1.** minor vomiting

_____ **2.** swallowing poison

_____ **3.** severe diarrhea

_____ **4.** runny nose

_____ **5.** diaper rash

_____ **6.** broken leg

_____ **7.** large cut from glass that won't stop bleeding

_____ **8.** swallowing a glass of milk

_____ **9.** a temperature of 104 degrees for an hour

_____**10.** severe stomachache

With the Screening Nurse

A. Hello. What's the patient's last name?

B. _____.

A. First name?

B. _____.

A. Age and date of birth?

B. _____.

A. Who's the regular doctor?

B. _____.

A. What's the problem?

B. _____.

A. Is there a fever or vomiting?

B. _____.

A. Any other symptoms?

B. _____.

A. Do you have insurance?

B. _____.

Required Information
for
Emergency Treatment

Please have this information ready for admission to the hospital.

1. Patient Information:

    a. Name _____

    b. Address _____

    c. Phone Number _____

2. Name of referring physician _____

3. Insurance Information:

    a. Policy Number or Group Number

    _____

    b. Social Security Number of employee

    _____

    c. Date of birth of employee _____

    d. Address of employee _____

    _____

4. Employment Information:

    a. Name _____

    b. Address _____

    c. Phone Number and Ext. _____

    d. Length of employment _____

A. My son broke his arm last night. The hospital bill was $800.

B. Do you have insurance?

A. Yes, I do. I'll use my health benefits at work. My insurance pays 100% of emergencies.

Check what can you do if you don't have health benefits.

_____ **1.** Call the Health Department. Ask what services are available.

_____ **2.** Get a job with benefits.

_____ **3.** Buy health insurance.

_____ **4.** Check to see if your wife or husband has benefits for the family.

_____ **5.** _____

_____

Talk about it.

1. Are there many doctors in your native country?

2. Was it easy to see a doctor in your native country?

3. Was it expensive to see a doctor in your native country?

Physicians

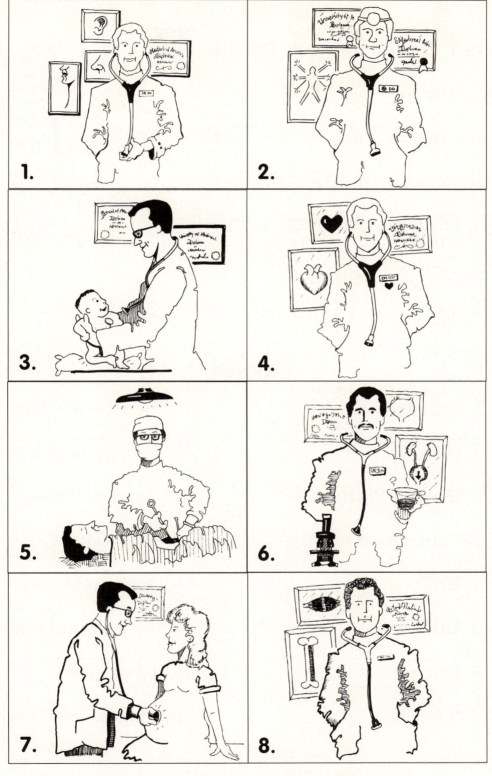

1.

2.

3.

4.

5.

6.

7.

8.

ENT-Ear, Nose, and Throat   General Practitioner
Pediatrician   Cardiologist
Surgeon   Urologist
OB-GYN   Orthopedist

A. What doctor are you here to see?

B. Dr. Jones.

A. He's an ENT doctor. What's wrong?

B. I have a sinus infection.

A. Oh, that can be very painful.

Match

____ 1. Pediatrician

____ 2. OB-GYN

____ 3. General Practitioner

____ 4. Cardiologist

____ 5. ENT

____ 6. Urologist

____ 7. Orthopedist

____ 8. Surgeon

a. hearing problems

b. general health problems

c. heart problems

d. for children

e. bone problems

f. for pregnant women

g. operations

h. bladder infections

Physicians

1. **A.** I'm going to see a _____.

   B. What's wrong?

   A. My heart beat is too fast.

2. **A.** I'm going to the_____.

   B. What's wrong?

   A. Nothing. I'm pregnant.

3. **A.** I'm going to the_____.

   B. What's wrong?

   A. I have a urinary tract infection.

4. **A.** I'm going to the_____.

   B. What's wrong?

   A. I'm going to have surgery.

5. **A.** I'm going to the_____.

   B. What's wrong?

   A. Nothing. My kids have check-ups.

6. **A.** I'm going to the _____.

   B. What's wrong?

   A. My tonsils are infected.

7. **A.** I'm going to the_____.

   B. What's wrong?

   A. I have a bad cold.

8. **A.** I'm going to the_____.

   B. What's wrong?

   A. I dislocated my knee playing basketball.

A. Excuse me, where's Dr. Oldmoney's office?

B. It's on the second floor.

A. Is there an elevator here?

B. Yes, go down the hall to the pharmacy. The elevator is on the left.

A. Would you repeat that please?

B. Go down the hall to the pharmacy. You'll see the elevator on the left.

A. Thanks.

Where's

| the elevator? |
| the drinking fountain? |
| the restroom? |

It's _____.

Complete the answers.

1. Where's the medicine for Pedro?

   Here's _____ _____.

2. Where's the message from Dr. Kaplan?

   Here's _____ _____ _____.

3. Where are the forms for Dr. Oldmoney?

   Here are _____ _____ _____.

4. Where's the immunization record for Fara?

   Here's _____ _____ _____.

5. Where's the X-ray for Steve?

   Here's _____ _____.

6. Where's the prescription for Mr. Ruiz?

   Here's _____ _____ _____.

7. Where are the insurance forms for Trevor?

   Here are _____ _____ _____.

8. Where are the test results for Erika?

   Here are _____ _____ _____.

9. Where's the chart for Lacey?

   Here's _____ _____.

10. Where are the lab results for Bill?

    Here are _____ _____ _____.

A. Hello. I'm Dr. Oldmoney.

B. Good morning.

A. What seems to be the problem?

B. I'm having trouble | breathing.
walking.
sleeping.
seeing.
eating.
hearing.

A. How long have you been feeling this way?

B. For a week.

A. How long has it been since your last physical?

B. I'm not sure, maybe several years.

A. It's probably time for a complete physical.

A. Let's start your physical.

B. O.K.

A. We need to take some tests. Can you go to the lab?

B. Sure, where is it?

A. It's upstairs next to Pediatrics.

FIRST FLOOR	SECOND FLOOR
100 GENERAL PRACTITIONER	200 EAR NOSE THROAT
101 OB GYN	201 PEDIATRICS
102 UROLOGY	203 LABORATORY
103 CARDIOLOGY	202 PHARMACY
104 SURGEON	204 ORTHOPEDIST

Check what you go to the lab for.

_____ **1.** a blood test

_____ **2.** a prescription

_____ **3.** a mammogram

_____ **4.** a baby

_____ **5.** a urine test

_____ **6.** an x-ray

_____ **7.** an immunization

_____ **8.** a sonogram

_____ **9.** an EKG

_____ **10.** a physical exam

```
+--------------------------------------------------------------+
|       FIRST FLOOR          SECOND FLOOR                      |
|                                                              |
|   100 GENERAL          200 EAR NOSE THROAT                   |
|       PRACTITIONER                                           |
|   101 OB GYN           201 PEDIATRICS                        |
|                                                              |
|   102 UROLOGY          203 LABORATORY                        |
|                                                              |
|   103 CARDIOLOGY       202 PHARMACY                          |
|                                                              |
|   104 SURGEON          204 ORTHOPEDIST                       |
|                                                              |
+--------------------------------------------------------------+
```

1. If you are pregnant, go to room _____.

2. If you need a prescription, go to room _____.

3. If you have heart problems, go to room _____.

4. If your children need check-ups, go to room _____.

5. If you are having an operation, go to room _____.

6. If it hurts to urinate, go to room _____.

7. If you have a bad ear infection, go to room _____.

8. If you need a blood test and an X-ray, go to room _____.

9. If you need a check-up, go to room _____.

10. If you have a problem with your hip, go to room _____.

Laughter is the Best Medicine

Adults have busy lives. We are busy taking care of our families and working. We worry about our children, money, and jobs. Life is stressful for everyone.

What happens to people with too much stress? Some people have high blood pressure, upset stomachs, and even heart disease. We know that eating good food and exercising are two ways to stay healthy. How can we reduce stress?

One easy way to reduce stress is to laugh more. Laughing helps us feel young. Laughing gives us energy. So it is important to take time for fun and laughter. We can plan to have fun.

Make a list of things that you like to do. Then do them. Remember, laughter is important. It is the best medicine.

Here are five words from the story. Underline them in the story. Use each in a new sentence.

1. worry _____

2. stressful _____

3. happens _____

4. laughter _____

5. energy _____

Finish these sentences.

1. One easy way to reduce stress is to _____ more.

2. _____ helps us feel young.

3. We know that eating good _____ and _____ are two ways to stay _____.

4. Laughing gives us _____.

5. It's _____ to take time for _____ and _____.

List five things you like to do:

1. _____

2. _____

3. _____

4. _____

5. _____

List five things you would like to try:

1. _____

2. _____

3. _____

4. _____

5. _____

A. I'm calling to get my test results.

B. O.K. The doctor will call you back. Your name please?

A. _____

B. What number can he reach you at?

A. _____

B. O.K. _____, the doctor will
name

return your call this afternoon.

A. Thank you.

The tests were: positive. +

negative. −

good.

borderline.

O.K.

not clear. We need to repeat them.

not ready.

A. Dr. Maltz's office.

B. Hello, this is _____. I have a question about my prescription.

A. Yes, what is it?

B. I'm not sure how long I need to take it. I feel fine now.

A. What does the prescription say?

B. It says to take it for ten days.

A. What's the medicine?

B. It's tetracycline.

A. It's very important to finish it all. You need to take it even when you're feeling better.

B. O.K. Thank you. I'll take it.

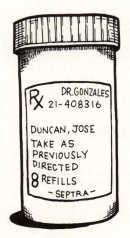

How much?   _____

When?   _____

What?   _____

How long?   _____

Who is it for?   _____

Who is the doctor?   _____

A. Kien's Pharmacy. Can I help you?

B. I want to refill my prescription.

A. What's the prescription number?

B. _____.

A. What's your name?

B. _____.

A. Spell that.

B. _____.

A. What's your doctor's name?

B. _____.

A. That will be ready in an hour.

B. Thanks.

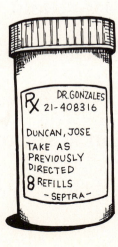

1.

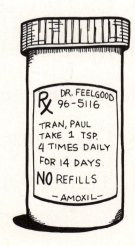

2.

Write the name and phone numbers of the hospital nearest you.

1. Local hospital name _____

2. 24–hour hospital number _____

3. Emergency room number _____

4. Patient information number _____

5. Hospital pharmacy number _____

6. Nearby 24 hour pharmacy number _____

A. Good morning. _____ Hospital.

B. Can you tell me how Bill Hartfield is doing?

A. Spell the last name, please.

B. H-A-R-T-F-I-E-L-D

A. One moment. His condition is serious but improving.

B. Thank you.

Fair	O.K.
Stable	↓
Serious	
Critical	bad
Guarded	

Circle which you think.

1. Her condition is serious.   Good   Bad

2. Her condition is critical.   Good   Bad

3. Her condition is fair.   Good   Bad

4. Her condition is stable.   Good   Bad

5. Her condition is serious but improving.   Good   Bad

6. Her condition is critical but improving.   Good   Bad

7. Her condition is serious but stable.   Good   Bad

8. Her condition is not stable.   Good   Bad

9. Her condition is fair and improving.   Good   Bad

10. Her condition is critical with no change.   Good   Bad

11. Her condition is guarded. The hospital   Good   Bad
    won't say if it's bad or good.

A. My friend is in the hospital.

B. I'm sorry to hear that. How's he doing?

A. He's doing O.K. I'm going to see him this morning.

B. I think visiting hours are in the afternoon and evening. They're from 2 to 5 p.m. and 6 to 8 p.m.

A. Thanks, I'll go tonight instead.

What time are the visting hours?

HOSPITAL VISITING HOURS

1ST FLOOR - PEDIATRICS
PARENTS - ANY TIME

2ND FLOOR - MATERNITY
FATHERS AND GRANDPARENTS - ANY TIME

3RD FLOOR
TWO (2) VISITORS AT A TIME
2:00 - 5:00 PM - 6:00 - 8:00 PM

4TH FLOOR
I.C.U., SURGERY AND RECOVERY
NO VISITORS

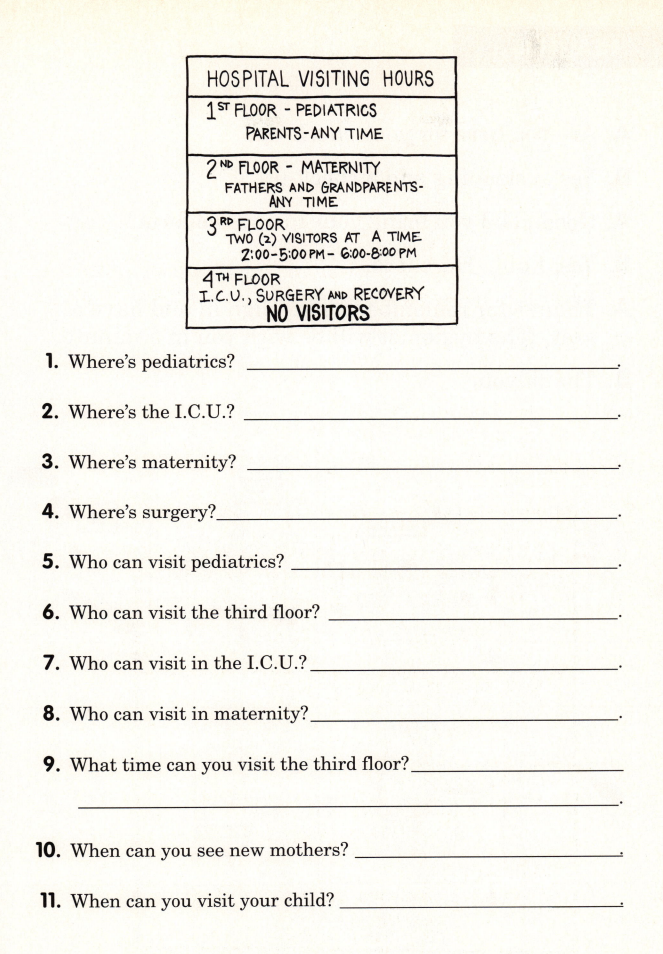

HOSPITAL VISITING HOURS

1ST FLOOR - PEDIATRICS
PARENTS-ANY TIME

2ND FLOOR - MATERNITY
FATHERS AND GRANDPARENTS-
ANY TIME

3RD FLOOR
TWO (2) VISITORS AT A TIME
2:00-5:00 PM - 6:00-8:00 PM

4TH FLOOR
I.C.U., SURGERY AND RECOVERY
NO VISITORS

1. Where's pediatrics? _____.

2. Where's the I.C.U.? _____.

3. Where's maternity? _____.

4. Where's surgery?_____.

5. Who can visit pediatrics? _____.

6. Who can visit the third floor? _____.

7. Who can visit in the I.C.U.?_____.

8. Who can visit in maternity?_____.

9. What time can you visit the third floor?_____

_____.

10. When can you see new mothers? _____.

11. When can you visit your child? _____.

A. Are you here for your check-up?

B. Yes, a cleaning and a check-up.

A. Good. Did you bring your insurance form?

B. Yes, I did. Here it is.

A. Thanks for remembering it. Sign in and have a seat. The hygienist will be with you in a minute.

B. Thank you.

1.   2.   3.   4.

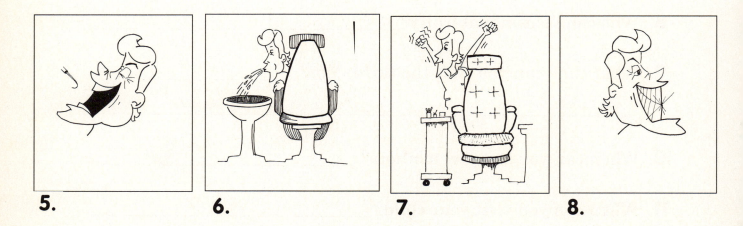

5.   6.   7.   8.

At the Dentist

A. Good morning, Mr. West.

B. Hi, Dr. Gold.

A. Have you had any problems?

B. Yes.
My gums have been sore.
My gums have been bleeding.
My gums have been swollen.
I have a toothache.
My tooth has bothered me.
My tooth broke.
My filling came out.
I think I have a cavity.
I think I have an infection.
It hurts to chew.

A. Let me take a look.

Circle **Yes** or **No**.

1. I've gone to the dentist.   Yes   No

2. I've had check-ups every six months.   Yes   No

3. I've had X-rays to check for cavities.   Yes   No

4. The hygienist has cleaned my teeth.   Yes   No

5. I've had fluoride treatments.   Yes   No

6. I've had cavities.   Yes   No

7. I've had a toothache.   Yes   No

8. To protect healthy teeth, everyone should   Yes   No
   visit the dentist.

9. I've had teeth pulled.   Yes   No

Copy the sentences that are true for you.

_____

_____

_____

_____

_____

_____

_____

4

SAFETY

A. Do you sell smoke detectors?

B. Yes, they're in the hardware department next to the fire extinquishers.

A. Thanks. Oh, do they need batteries?

B. Yes, check the instructions on the box.

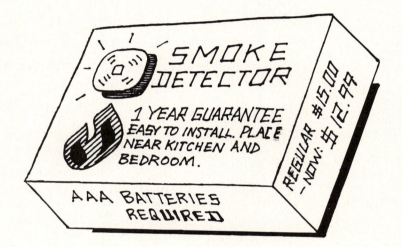

1. How much is the smoke detector? _____.

2. How long is it guaranteed to work. _____.

3. Where do you install the smoke detector? _____

_____

4. Can you install it yourself? _____.

5. What kind of batteries does it use? _____.

6. How do you know when to replace the batteries? _____

_____.

A Family Saved

There was a fire in a mobile home. Inside the home, the family was sleeping. As smoke filled the mobile home the mother woke up.

The family didn't have a smoke detector, but the mother smelled the smoke. She woke up her husband. He went to rescue their two children while she broke a window.

The mother got out quickly through the window. The father was going to hand her the children through the window.

A neighbor saw the fire and ran over to help. He went inside the burning home. He found one child quickly. He carried the child to the mother. Then he went back inside and found the father. The father was unconscious on the floor. The neighbor pulled him to a broken window and pushed him out.

Now, there was one more child to save, a ten-week old baby. The neighbor looked, but the smoke was very thick. He couldn't find the baby. Finally, the neighbor found the baby.

The mother, father, two children, and the neighbor all had to go to the hospital. The neighbor was a hero. He saved three lives.

This family didn't have a smoke detector, but they do now.

1. What would you do if you saw a fire?

_____

2. Do you have a smoke detector? _____

Reread the story. Underline the words you don't know.
Answer the questions below about the story.

1. Who woke up and smelled smoke?_____

2. Who was rescued last? _____

3. Who saved three people in this story? _____

4. Where was the fire? _____

5. Where did the father go? _____

6. Where did the mother go?_____

7. How old were the children?_____

8. How many people lived in the mobile home? _____

9. Why do you think the father was unconscious? _____

10. Why did the family go to the hospital?_____

_____

11. Why is the neighbor a hero?_____

12. Do you know someone who is a hero? _____

13. Who is your hero? _____

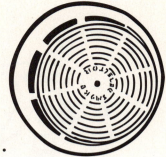

A. Hello. I'm the tenant in apartment 3.

B. Yes, I know. What can I do for you?

A. Have you checked the smoke detectors recently? I'm not sure mine is working.

B. I'll check yours today. They should be working in every apartment.

1. Do you have a smoke detector? _____

2. Have you checked it recently? _____

3. Have you replaced its battery recently? _____

4. Have you heard the alarm from the smoke detector? _____

5. Have you disconnected your smoke detector? _____

Be Safe, Not Sorry

In case of fire you should have a fire extinguisher in your home.

You can buy a fire extinguisher at _____.

You should keep one near your stove and one in your garage.

A fire extinguisher costs about _____.

To use a fire extinguisher, you do three things:
1. Pull the pin.
2. Squeeze the handle.
3. Spray side to side.

To use a fire extinguisher:

1. First, you _____.

2. Second, you _____.

3. Third, you _____.

A House Fire

1. In case of fire you should crawl to the door.

2. In case of fire you should call from a neighbor's house.

3. You should have a smoke detector near the kitchen or the hall.

4. If there is a fire, touch the door panel. If it is hot, do not open the door.

5. You should keep a fire extinguisher in your home.

6. In case of fire you should _____ _____ _____ _____.

First Aid for a Burn

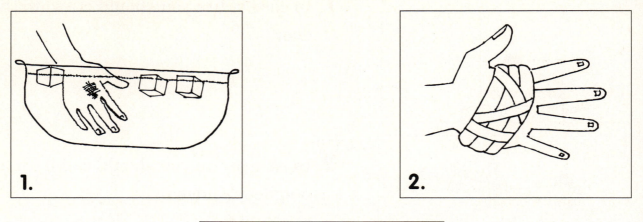

DO:

1. Place burned area in cool water. Do not soak longer than 30 minutes.

2. Cover the burn loosely with a clean bandage or cloth.

3. Call the doctor, or go to the hospital for all bad burns.

DO NOT:

1. Do not put butter, ointments, or grease on burns.

2. Do not remove anything sticking to the burn.

3. Do not break any blisters.

The First Aid Kit

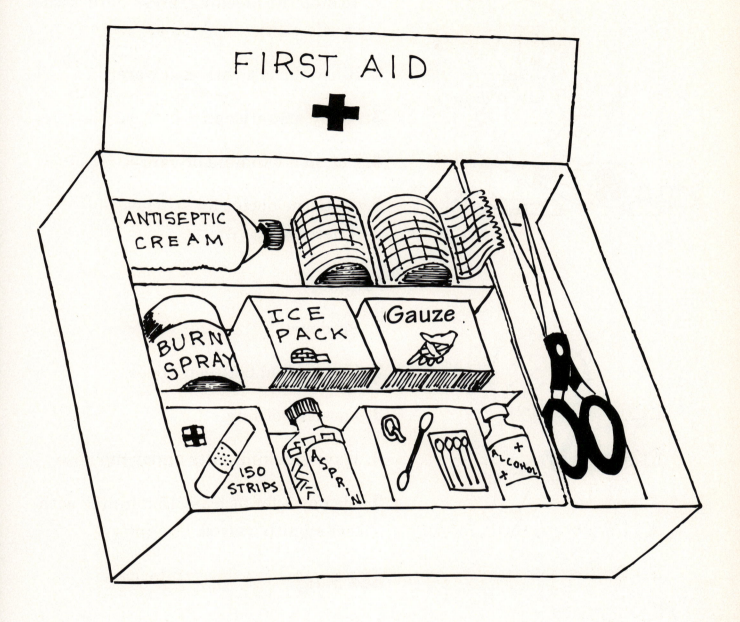

Simple First Aid Techniques

A Cut

1. To stop the bleeding, press hard with a sterile cloth.

2. Rinse the cut with cold water.

3. Apply an antiseptic.

4. Put on a band-aid or gauze.

5. Go to the doctor for stitches, if necessary.

Fainting

1. Sit down.

2. Lower head between knees.

3. Loosen clothing.

4. Wave smelling salts under the nose.

5. Lie down for at least 15 minutes with feet slightly raised.

Bee Sting

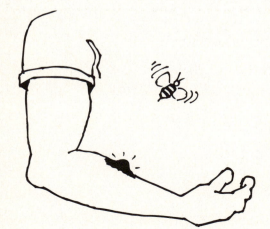

1. Put ice on the bee sting.

2. Take out the stinger.

3. Call your doctor if the victim gets sick. If allergic to a sting get to the hospital immediately.

The Storage Room

1. cleaning supplies
2. batteries
3. candles
4. flashlight
5. blankets
6. sleeping bags
7. cooler
8. can opener
9. bottled water
10. radio
11. canned food
12. suitcase
13. tools
14. _____

Natural Disasters: Earthquakes, Hurricanes, Floods and Tornadoes

There are always natural disasters. They occur all around the world. We never know what may happen or when, but we can be prepared. In case of any natural disaster you should have the following supplies:

1. extra drinking water in bottles
2. candles and matches, or a flashlight with extra batteries
3. a supply of canned food and a can opener
4. a radio with batteries
5. blankets and extra clothes
6. first aid supplies

Check what you have: Yes   No

1. bottled water   _____   _____

2. candles and matches or
   a flashlight with extra batteries   _____   _____

3. extra canned food and
   a can opener   _____   _____

4. prescription numbers of my medicines.   _____   _____

5. a radio with batteries   _____   _____

6. extra blankets and clothes   _____   _____

7. a first aid kit   _____   _____

I need to get _____

_____

Keep the items in a box you can take with you.

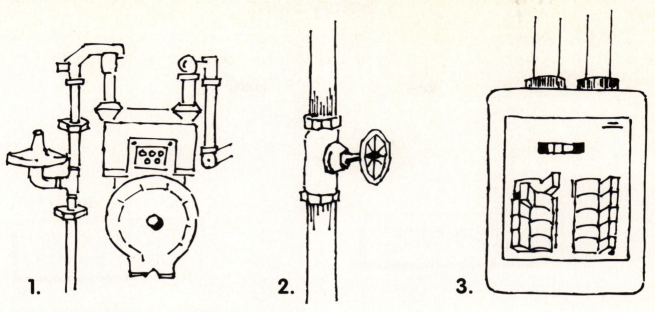

1.   **2.**   **3.**

Look for these in your home.

1. the gas valve
2. the main water valve
3. the circuit breaker or the fuse box

Learn how to turn off all utilities. If you live in an apartment, your manager will probably turn everything off in the building. Keep important phone numbers near your phone.

Manager's phone _____

Police, Fire, Emergency _____

Hospital _____

Doctor _____

Gas company _____

Children's school _____

Husband/wife at work _____

Safety Signs

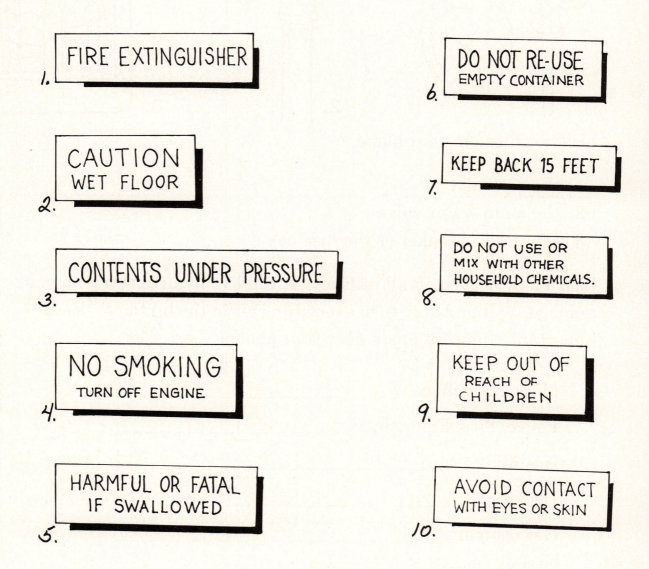

1. FIRE EXTINGUISHER

2. CAUTION WET FLOOR

3. CONTENTS UNDER PRESSURE

4. NO SMOKING TURN OFF ENGINE

5. HARMFUL OR FATAL IF SWALLOWED

6. DO NOT RE-USE EMPTY CONTAINER

7. KEEP BACK 15 FEET

8. DO NOT USE OR MIX WITH OTHER HOUSEHOLD CHEMICALS.

9. KEEP OUT OF REACH OF CHILDREN

10. AVOID CONTACT WITH EYES OR SKIN

A. Do you have car seats for babies?

B. We have several different sizes. How big is the baby?

A. He's two weeks old.

B. O.K. Let me show you a car seat for newborns.

NOT ONLY SAFE BUT SMART! HEAVY STRAPS SECURE SEAT TO CAR. HOLDS UP TO 20 POUNDS. $76.00

EASILY ADJUSTS TO GROWTH. SURPASSES ALL GOVERNMENT SAFETY STANDARDS. HOLDS UP TO 40 POUNDS. $89.00

Car Seats

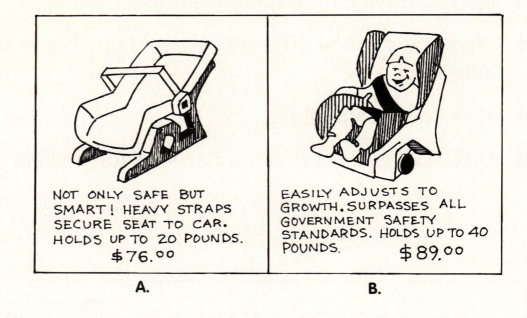

NOT ONLY SAFE BUT SMART! HEAVY STRAPS SECURE SEAT TO CAR. HOLDS UP TO 20 POUNDS. $76.00

A.

EASILY ADJUSTS TO GROWTH. SURPASSES ALL GOVERNMENT SAFETY STANDARDS. HOLDS UP TO 40 POUNDS. $89.00

B.

1. Which car seat holds up to 20 pounds? _____

2. Which car seat is government approved? _____

3. Which car seat is cheaper? _____

4. Your son weighs 25 pounds. Which car seat should he use?

_____

The Gift

Here's a story about a loving father. He gave his baby a gift. What do you think it was?

Lin bought his new baby girl a present. It was very expensive, and some relatives thought it was silly. He bought his beautiful baby girl a car seat.

His brother laughed at him. But his brother was single and didn't have any children. Lin said he would do anything for this baby, his first child.

A few months later Lin, his wife, and baby girl were driving to his mother's. The baby was strapped safely in her new seat. Lin and his wife were seat belted safely in their old car. Lin stopped at a red light. The baby was cooing in the back seat. Lin and his wife were talking about the future and the plans they had for their baby.

The light changed to green. Lin started across the intersection. What happened next was not Lin's fault. His car was hit by another car. The driver didn't stop at the red light. Lin and his wife weren't hurt. They were wearing seat belts. And the baby—well the baby was still cooing in the back seat. She wasn't hurt at all.

Now Lin tells everyone to strap their children in car seats. His little daughter will never know how lucky she was. But really, she was more than lucky. She had parents who loved her enough to strap her in the car seat.

1. Do you buy presents for new babies? _____

2. What is the best type of gift you can buy?_____

_____

Here are five words from the story. Underline them in the story. Use them in a new sentence.

1. silly _____

2. cooing _____

3. future _____

4. strap _____

5. accident _____

Reread the story. Write the answers.

1. Who bought the car seat? _____

2. Where was the accident? _____

3. Whose fault was the accident? _____

4. Why did Lin buy a car seat? _____

5. What does this sentence from the story mean: "But really, she was more than lucky?" _____

_____

Talk about it.

What is the law in your state about children and car seats?

Does the law apply to you?

IMPORTANT!   URGENT!

Dear Parents,

    This morning one of our students was hit by a car. The child will be fine, but we need to tell our children again to stay on the sidewalks, cross only in crosswalks or at corners, and to walk not run, to and from school. Please talk to your children about this very important matter.

Thank you,
Washington School
Faculty and School

Tell your children:

1. Stay on the sidewalk.
2. _____
3. _____
4. _____
5. _____

Safety Rules

Talk about it. Then complete each sentence.

1. Always cross the street at crosswalks or at signals so

    _____

2. Always wear seat belts because _____

    _____

3. Know your local emergency number so that _____

    _____

    _____

4. Check your smoke alarm because_____

    _____

5. Use a light on your bike at night so _____

    _____

6. Walk in lighted areas at night so that_____

    _____

7. Check the pilot lights on the stove because _____

    _____

8. Keep a fire extinguisher next to your stove because _____

    _____

9. Pull to the side when you hear a fire truck so that_____

    _____

10. You don't drink alcohol and drive because

    _____

11.   Repair frayed electrical cords so that

    _____

12. Keep small children in car seats so that_____

    _____

5

MESSAGES

Phone Calls

#1

A. Hello.

B. Hello, is Juana there?

A. Yes, this is Juana.

#2

A. Hello.

B. Hello, is Juana there?

A. I'm not sure. Let me check.

#3

A. Hello.

B. Hello, is Juana there?

A. Yes, just a minute. I'll get her.

#4

A. Hello.

B. Hello, is Juana there?

A. No, she isn't. Can I take a message?

B. Yes, please tell her _____ called. I'll call her back later.

Subject pronouns	Object pronouns
I you he, she, it we *They*	me you him, her, it us *them*

Choose the correct pronoun.

1. I called my brother, but _____ wasn't home.

2. My brother called you, but _____ weren't home.

3. She called me, but _____ wasn't home.

4. We called them, but _____ .

5. They called us, but _____ .

6. We called Juana, but _____ .

7. He called his boss, but _____ .

8. Tom called _____, but I _____ .

9. They called _____, but she _____ .

10. May called _____, but he _____ .

11. Grandfather called _____, but you _____ .

12. She called _____, but we _____ .

13. I called _____, but they _____ .

14. *You* Tú called _____, but we _____ .

What are these numbers?

1. _____ 411

a. operator–assisted long distance call; you pay

2. _____ 911

b. time

3. _____ 92111

c. operator

4. _____ 0-513-778-5670

d. direct–dial long distance; you pay

5. _____ 853-1212

e. social security number

6. _____ 1-800-555-5678

f. emergency police number

7. _____ 239-76-0462

g. zip code

8. _____ 1-281-555-5678

h. caller doesn't pay

9. _____ 0

i. information

• •

10. The local poison control number is: _____ – _____

11. My school office number is: _____ – _____

411 Information

A. What city?

B. Miami

A. Go ahead.

B. What's the number of Miami Day School?

A. The number is 555–4296. Once again, that's 555–4296.
Please make a note of it.

• •

Dictation. Listen and write the number.

1. _____

2. _____

3. _____

4. _____

5. _____

6. _____

7. _____

8. _____

A Message

TO **Mr. Smith**

DATE **4-8**   TIME **9:20**

WHILE YOU WERE OUT

MR. (MS) **Nguyen**

TELEPHONED

MESSAGE: **She wants to talk about her son's grade. Please call her back.**

Lena Garcia

1. Who's the message for?_____

2. Who's the message from? _____

3. Who took the message? _____

4. What time was the message taken? _____

5. What does Mrs. Nguyen want? _____

6. Do you think Mr. Smith will return her call? _____

7. Why or why not? _____

_____

Listen to your instructor and take a message.

TO _____

DATE _____ TIME ____

WHILE YOU WERE OUT

MR/MS _____

TELEPHONED

MESSAGE _____

_____

_____

_____

_____

1.

TO _____

DATE _____ TIME ____

WHILE YOU WERE OUT

MR/MS _____

TELEPHONED

MESSAGE _____

_____

_____

_____

_____

2.

A. Hello.

B. Hi. This is Lee. Is Kim there?

A. Kim? Kim who?

B. Kim Perez.

A. No, sorry. I think you have the wrong number.

B. Is this 555-2149?

A. No, it isn't.

B. Oh, sorry to bother you.

A. That's O.K.

Write the complete response. Begin all responses with *No.*

1. A. Is Effat there?
  B. (not here) _____

2. A. Is Grandpa there?
  B. (wrong number) _____

3. A. Is the nurse there?
  B. (call you back)_____

Telephone Calls

Write the complete response. Begin all responses with either *Yes* or *No*.

1. A. Hello. Is Dr. Paul there?

   B. (out of town) _____

2. A. Is Mrs. Lue there?

   B. (just a minute) _____

3. A. Is the pharmacist there?

   B. (busy) _____

4. A. Is Miss Garza there?

   B. (on the other line–wait) _____

5. A. Is the attendance clerk there?

   B. (call him later) _____

6. A. Is the school principal there?

   B. (call back at 2:00 p.m.)_____

7. A. Is the manager there?

   B. (leave a message)_____

8. A. Is Franco there?

   B. (moved) _____

9. A. Is Leticia there?

   B. (new number)_____

Work as partners. Partner A uses this page. Partner A reads Message #1. Partner B uses the next page. Partner B fills in the form. Partner A may read the message again if necessary. Repeat for Message #2, then trade tasks.

Message #1

It's 2:20. This is radio station 91 X. You have won two movie tickets. Call 555-7091 to get them.

Message #2

Hello, it's 9:00. This is Mrs. Smith, your son's teacher. I wanted to tell you how well your son is doing in school. The office number is 251-6003.

Message #3

Mary, this is Sue, down the street. I need to borrow your dictionary tonight. It's 7:30. Call me at 596-3287.

Message #4

Hello, this is Pat from the office. You need to fill in some forms for your insurance. Call me tomorrow at 876-9081. It's 1:20 now.

Take a Message

Student B uses this page

Message #1

Who called? _____   What time? _____

Return number? _____

Message? _____

_____

Message #2

Who called? _____   What time? _____

Return number? _____

Message? _____

_____

Message #3

Who called? _____   What time? _____

Return number? _____

Message? _____

_____

Message #4

Who called? _____   What time? _____

Return number? _____

Message? _____

_____

The Answering Machine

Leave a message on a telephone answering machine. Remember to include:

1. Your name
2. The time of your call
3. Your reason for calling
4. Your phone number

A. Hi. This is Mary. We're unable to answer the phone now, so please leave a message at the beep. Thank you.

BEEP

B. _____

_____

_____

_____

_____

_____

_____

_____

_____

_____

Look at the illustration on the previous page and answer these questions.

1. How many bedrooms does the house have? _____

2. What numbers would you call if you needed a place to live?

   _____

3. Who can attend the parenting film?_____

4. Where is the grand opening? _____

5. What is the date of the grand opening? _____

6. What number do you call for information on the trip to Hollywood?

   _____

7. When can you call about the refrigerator? _____

8. Where is the film on parenting? _____

9. When is the senior citizen trip?_____

10. What number do you call to trade a used car for a motorcycle?

    _____

11. Who can take the bus trip to Hollywood? _____

    _____

12. Why would you call 921-6091? _____

    _____

A. I need a baby stroller. I'd like to find a good used one.

B. Have you looked on the bulletin board at the

> supermarket?
> library?
> school?
> community center?
> _____?

A. No, I haven't. I didn't think of that.

B. Sometimes there are real bargains.

A. Thanks, I'll try that.

Check where you might find a community bulletin board.

____ at a school
____ at a supermarket
____ at a doctor's office
____ at a gas station
____ at a community center
____ at a library
____ at the video store
____ at a bank

Check what you might find advertised on a community bulletin board.

____ a house for rent
____ a stroller for sale
____ a job
____ a wife
____ childbirth classes
____ a free lotto ticket
____ a car for sale

A. Can I put my ad on your bulletin board?

B. Certainly. What's it for?

A. I'm selling my truck. It's a '79 Toyota pick-up. I'm asking $1,100.

B. Is it in good condition?

A. Yes.

B. How many miles are on it?

A. 91,000.

B. Good luck.

A. Thanks.

The phone number is 555-6210. Write the ad to sell the truck.

_____

_____

_____

_____

_____

_____

Write an ad to sell the item. Include a telephone number, time to call, and condition of the item. You may include a name and price, too.

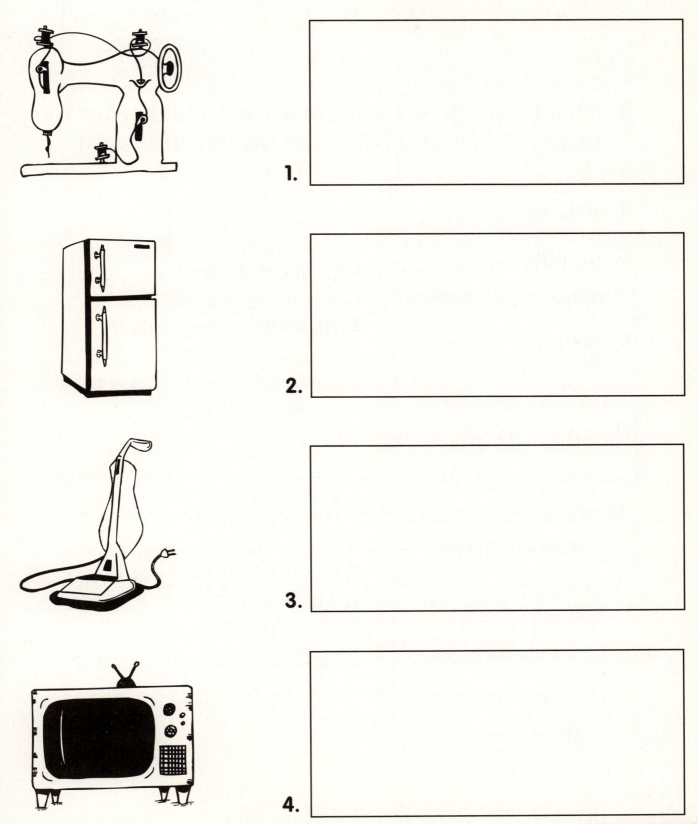

1.

2.

3.

4.

A. Congratulations. You finished your

> typing
> auto-repair
> sewing
> cooking

class.

B. Thank you. Now I want to use my skill to earn some money. I'm putting an ad on the bulletin board.

Read the ads:

Dressmaking and Alterations

Zippers	$5
Hems	$7

I can make it like you want it!

Rosa   555–9734

1. What can she sew? _____

2. Who do you ask for? _____

3. What's the phone number?

_____

4. How much does she charge to put in a zipper? _____

Minor Auto Repair

Oil change	$15
tune ups	$25

ask for Joel at

525–8124

1. What's the ad for?

_____

2. How much are oil changes? _____

3. Who do you call? _____

4. What's the phone number?

_____

Write the questions.

TYPING
ANY KIND FROM
$2.00 A PAGE
MAI: 292-8762

a. _____?

Any kind

b. _____?

$2 a page

c. _____?

292-8762

d. _____?

Ask for Mai.

AUTO REPAIR
FREE ESTIMATE.
CHEAPEST IN TOWN. I
CAN FIX ANYTHING
QUOC: 521-9372

e. _____?

Anything

f. _____?

Lowest prices

g. _____?

521-9372

h. _____?

Ask for Quoc.

ALTERATIONS
CALL SUE: 555-9110
AFTER 9:AM
$2.00 HEM IN DRESS
$3.00 PANTS HEM
$5.00 ZIPPER REPAIR

i. _____?

$5

j. _____?

After 9 a.m.

k. _____?

555-9110

l. _____?

Ask for Sue.

CHINESE CATERING
DIM SUM IN YOUR
HOME FOR 5 TO 500
PEOPLE.
CHANG LE 971-6230

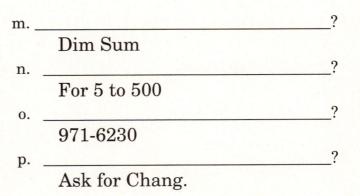

m. _____?

Dim Sum

n. _____?

For 5 to 500

o. _____?

971-6230

p. _____?

Ask for Chang.

Yes or No

Ask your classmate the question. Check if the answer is **Yes**; leave blank if the answer is **No**.

Have you_____?

_____**1.** called 911?

_____**2.** used 411?

_____**3.** dialed 0?

_____**4.** called long distance?

_____**5.** called for time check?

_____**6.** used an 800 number?

_____**7.** talked to a telephone operator?

_____**8.** dialed the wrong number?

_____**9.** called a 900 number?

_____**10.** used a pay phone?

_____**11.** taken a phone message?

_____**12.** read the phone book?

_____**13.** called out of the United States?

_____**14.** left a message on an answering machine?

_____**15.** called another country?

6

JOBS

A. What jobs have you had?

B. I've been a _____.

A. What job would you like to have?

B. I would like to_____.

A. Do you know how much it pays?

B. I think it pays about _____ an hour.
I think it pays about _____ a week.
I think it pays about _____ a month.
I think it pays about _____ a year.

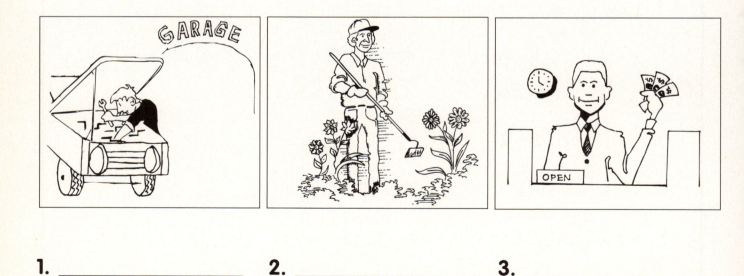

1. _____ 2. _____ 3. _____

The President of the United States

Do you know how much the president of the United States earns a year? The U.S. president has an important job. He works long hours, seven days a week. Even on vacation he is responsible for our country. He earns his salary. These are the salaries for this job since 1789. George Washington and Herbert Hoover did not accept their salaries. John F. Kennedy donated his salary to charity.

	Year	Salary
1.	1789	$25,000
2.	1883	$50,000
3.	1909	$75,000
4.	1949	$100,000
5.	1969	$200,000
6.	1988	$200,000
7.	now	_____

Questions:

1. How much did the president earn in 1949? _____

2. How much did the first U.S. president, George Washington, earn?

   _____

3. How much did the president earn in 1909? _____

4. What kind of job does the president have? _____

5. Which presidents didn't accept their salary?_____

6. Which president donated his salary to charity? _____

A. It's difficult to get a job.

B. Yes, it is. You need to have some kind of skill or training.

A. You usually need some previous experience, too.

What skills do you have?

1. _____

2. _____

3. _____

4. _____

What is your previous experience?

1. _____

2. _____

3. _____

4. _____

Kinds of Jobs

Not everyone has the experience to be President of the United States. But we are all able to take job-training courses to teach us skills for other jobs.

Match these job titles with the pictures on the next page.

Picture Number

_____ **1.** small–appliance repair person

_____ **2.** landscaping

_____ **3.** bank teller

_____ **4.** veterinarian's assistant

_____ **5.** dry cleaner

_____ **6.** data entry clerk

_____ **7.** nurse

_____ **8.** beautician

_____ **9.** medical lab assistant

_____ **10.** bookkeeper

_____ **11.** food service worker

_____ **12.** pre-school worker

Talk about it.

1. What jobs interest you?

2. What skills do the jobs need?

3. How much money do the jobs pay?

Job Training

Job	Salary per hour	Salary per year
Beautician	$9.00	$18,000
Doctor		$130,000
President of the U.S.		$200,000
Data Entry	$7.00	$14,163
Landscaper	$8.75	$17,500
Bookkeeper	$10.50	$21,000
Librarian	$15.00	$30,000
Medical Lab Assistant	$12.00	$24,000
Baseball Pitcher		$3,000,000
Dry Cleaning Worker	$6.50	$13,000
Actor		$20,000,000
Truck Driver	$12.50	$25,000
Bank Teller	$8.00	$16,640
School Principal		$42,000

1. How much does the president earn per year? _____

2. How much does an actor earn per year? _____

3. How much does a beautician earn per hour? _____

4. How much does a bank teller earn per hour? _____

5. Does a school principal earn more than a landscaper? _____

6. Does a medical lab assistant earn more than a truck driver?

_____

7. Who earns the least, a landscaper or a librarian? _____

A. How do I apply for job training?

B. You need to come in to our counseling office. A counselor here will help you.

A. Do I need an appointment?

B. No, you don't. Come anytime between 8:00 A.M. and 8:30 P.M. We're open Monday through Friday.

Match the skills with the occupations. An occupation may require more than one skill.

1. _____ bank teller
2. _____ beautician
3. _____ food service worker
4. _____ bookkeeper
5. _____ small appliance repair worker
6. _____ medical lab assistant
7. _____ child care and preschool worker
8. _____ landscaper

a. making change
b. reading numbers
c. understanding math
d. preparing food
e. following directions
f. handling difficult people
g. loving children
h. enjoy working outside

List three things each person does.

1. _____

2. _____

3. _____

4. _____

5. _____

6. _____

7. _____

8. _____

9. _____

10. _____

11. _____

12. _____

13. _____

14. _____

15. _____

JOB TRAINING APPLICATION

1. Name: _____
                last   first   middle

2. Address: _____
          no.   street   city   state zip

3. Age: _____ No. of years in U.S. _____

4. Have you had job training before?   no ☐
                                           yes ☐

5. Have you worked in the U.S. before?   no ☐
                                           yes ☐

6. If #5 is yes, what was your job? _____

7. List previous experience: _____

_____

8. How many years' experience do you have? _____

9. What job training would you like? _____

_____

10. Do you have a   _____ GED

                          _____ High School Diploma

                          _____ AA Degree

                          _____ Four Year Degree

                          _____ Other _____

A. I'm looking for a job .

B. How long have you been looking?

A. I've been looking for several weeks.

B. You could try _____. They're interviewing.

A. Really? What do I do?

1. Get an application.
2. Fill out the application.
3. Make an appointment for an interview.
4. Look your best for the interview.
5. Practice the handshake for the interview.
6. Learn about the job you want.

A. Have you found a job yet?

B. I'm still looking. Today I'm going to an electronics firm. I've heard they're hiring.

A. Do you have to fill out an application?

B. I'm sure I do.

A. Do you have to have an interview?

B. Probably.

A. How about a resume? Do you have to have one?

B. Gee, I don't know.

Places to look for jobs

1. _____

2. _____

3. _____

4. _____

5. _____

A. I'd like to apply for the welding job.

B. Fill out this application. Leave it with the secretary. If you have a resume you can leave it, too.

PERSONAL

Print or Type All Requested Information

Position Applying For: _____

Name _____
　　　　Last　　　　　　　First　　　　　　　Middle

Address _____
　　　Street　　　City　　　State　　Zip　　Phone

Social Security Number: _____ Are you over 18 years of age? _____ Date Available _____

AVAILABILITY

List hours available for work:　　　　　　　Salary expected: _____

	Sun.	M	T	W	Th	F	Sat.
DAY							
NIGHT							

Total Weekly
Hours Desired _____

How will you get to work? _____

EDUCATION

Circle last grade completed:

Grade 5 6 7 8　　High School 1 2 3 4　　College 1 2 3 4

Name and address of last school attended: _____ _____

Special Skills and Training: _____
_____

_____　　　_____
　　　Date　　　　　　　　　　　Applicant's Signature

A resume tells about your education and experience. You can list all your skills and special achievements. References are the names of people who will recommend you for the job.

Resume

John Black
9808 Green Road
New York, NY 91101

Education:

1987-1988	North City Adult School
1988-1990	North City Job Training
1990	North City Welding Certificate

Job Experience:

1987-1988	Janitor Service, Inc.–night janitor
1988-1989	Bill's Auto Body– painting and sanding
1989-present	Amco Steel and Shipbuilding–welder's assistant

References:	Furnished upon request

1. What is John's experience? _____

_____

2. What job did he have from 1987 to 1988?

_____

3. Where did John go to school from 1988-1990? _____

_____

4. What job does he have now?_____

_____

The Interview

A. Come in and have a seat. How are you?

B. Fine, thanks. How are you?

A. Fine, too. Tell me about your job experience.

B. I was a welder for five years in my country.

A. That's good. Do you have any questions about the job?

B. Yes, I do. When does the job start?

You should ask at least two questions during the interview. This shows you are really interested in the job.

Match the questions with the answers.

1. How much does the job pay? _____   a. 8–5 with a 1 hour lunch

2. Is it full-time or part time? _____   b. $7.50 an hour.

3. What are the hours? _____   c. Tuesday through Sunday, full-time

4. What are the benefits? _____   d. White shoes and an apron

5. Is a uniform worn? _____   e. 1–week paid vacation

6. What equipment do I need? _____   f. We provide all the tools.

Job	Where	Salary	Hours	Benefits
Data Entry	ABC Corp.	$1200 mo.	M-F 7-4 full-time	health insurance & 1 week vacation
Child care Worker	Humpty Dumpty	$5.50 hr.	20 hr. per week	no benefits
Food Service	Milton Hotel	$1100 mo.	part-time 20-30 hrs. per week	some benefits
Medical Lab Assistant	New Design Inc.	$12.50 hr.	full-time	health and dental sick leave 2 wks. vacation

1. Where is the data entry job? _____

2. Where is the medical lab assistant job? _____

3. How much is the salary for the child care worker? _____

4. How much does the food service job pay? _____

5. What job has no benefits? _____

6. Which jobs have health benefits? _____

7. What jobs are full time? _____

8. What job has the best benefits? _____

9. What job is at the Milton Hotel? _____

TASTEE DONUTS
Part time job.
Openings AM or PM
call   555-9736

A. I'm calling about the job ad in the paper.

B. Yes, we need someone to help in a donut shop.
It's easy work, part time, and fun. Are you
interested?

A. I think so, but I have some questions.

Write the questions.   Answers

1. _____   Minimum wage.

2. _____   Every two weeks.

3. _____   10:00 P.M. to 2:00 A.M.

4. _____   Tastee Donuts.

5. _____   Beach area.

6. _____   No benefits.

7. _____   Immediately.

1. Do you have a job now? ____

2. Do you have a break on your job? ____

On the Job

Sometimes it's difficult for people to meet people when they start a new job. Break time is a good time to meet new people. Employees take breaks in the cafeteria, the employee lounge, or outside the building.

Americans share many things about themselves with the people they work with. We talk about our families, our ideas, the news, and the weather. During your break time, feel free to join in the conversations.

Talk about it.

Here are some comments you might hear at work. What are some responses you can make to them?

1. A. This weather is hot.

B. _____

2. A. My kids are driving me nuts.

B. _____

3. A. I'm ready for a vacation.

B. _____

4. A. I need a better car.

B. _____

5. A. My son is getting married.

B. _____

Your Paycheck

EARNINGS				DEDUCTIONS			WARRANT NUMBER 93- 251113
TYPE	HOURS	RATE	AMOUNT	TYPE	YEAR TO DATE	CURRENT	
clerk	80	12	960	Fed Tax	192.40	96.20	SOCIAL SECURITY NO. 221-58-0672
				Cal Tax	19.20	9.60	
				Hlth Ins.	104.	52.00	PERIOD ENDING 1-28-95

TAXABLE GROSS							
TYPE	YEAR TO DATE	CURRENT					LEAVE BALANCES Vacation 00 Sick Leave 5 days
Gross	1920	960.00					
				GROSS PAY 960.00 TOTAL DEDUCTIONS 157.80 NET PAY 802.20			

1. Does this person have benefits? _____

2. Does this person pay federal income tax? _____

3. Does this person pay state income tax? _____

4. Does this person pay health insurance? _____

5. What's the gross pay? _____

6. What's the net pay? _____

Rene made a mistake. What was his mistake? Read and find out.

Rene's Job

Rene had a job downtown. He chopped vegetables and made salads for a large hotel restaurant. He worked full-time. He worked from two in the afternoon until closing.

He liked his job and his friends there. Rene had worked in the restaurant for four months.

One day he didn't feel well, but he went to work anyway. Two days later he felt worse. He went to the doctor on his day off. The doctor said, "Rene, you must go home and go to bed. You have the flu."

So Rene did what the doctor said. He went home and went to bed. He watched TV and drank juice. He rested but he didn't call his work. The next week Rene felt better. He returned to work, but more bad news. He was fired! His boss was angry. He said, "Rene, where have you been? We needed you."

Here are five words from the story. Underline them in the story.
Use each in a new sentence.

1. anyway _____

2. worse _____

3. flu _____

4. felt _____

5. fired _____

Talk about it:

1. What was Rene's job?

2. What happened to Rene?

3. What was Rene's mistake?

4. What could he have done?

A. Viva la France Restaurant. Can I help you?

B. Hello, this is _____. Is the boss there?

A. No he isn't. He'll be back in ten minutes. Can I take a message?

B. No. I'll call back in ten minutes. I need to tell him I'm too sick to work tonight.

A. O.K. Hope you feel better.

B. Thanks. Good-bye.

Check the valid reasons why you might miss work.

_____ **1.** I have a little cold.

_____ **2.** I have car trouble.

_____ **3.** My wife had a baby yesterday.

_____ **4.** I need to go shopping.

_____ **5.** I want to go fishing.

_____ **6.** I have the chicken pox.

_____ **7.** I have a mild headache.

_____ **8.** I want to paint my living room.

7

SPENDING WISELY

A. What would you buy if you had an extra $10.00?

B. I don't know. I'd have to think about it.
What would you buy?

A. If I had an extra $10.00 I'd buy | lunch.
a book.
a pizza.

Ask your classmates: "What would you buy if you had an extra $10.00?"

Name	Item
1. _____	
2. _____	
3. _____	
4. _____	

Write what you found out in sentences:

1. If _____ had an extra $10.00 _____

_____

2. _____

_____

3. _____

_____

4. _____

_____

Checks

Write each number.

_____ one	_____ eleven	_____ thirty
_____ two	_____ twelve	_____ forty
_____ three	_____ thirteen	_____ fifty
_____ four	_____ fourteen	_____ sixty
_____ five	_____ fifteen	_____ seventy
_____ six	_____ sixteen	_____ eighty
_____ seven	_____ seventeen	_____ ninety
_____ eight	_____ eighteen	_____ one hundred
_____ nine	_____ nineteen	_____ one thousand
_____ ten	_____ twenty	_____ one million

Write the correct amounts.

1. $19.36

Illinois Trust & Savings Bank
6193 Broadway
Park Ridge, IL 60068

1118
16-21/1222

_____ 19 _____

Pay to
the Order Of _____ $ _____

DOLLARS

LACY WEST
2299 FIRST STREET
PARK RIDGE, IL 60068
MEMO _____

1 1 2200 520 370 204 4323 111

2. $78.52

Illinois Trust & Savings Bank
6193 Broadway
Park Ridge, IL 60068

1118
16-21/1222

_____ 19 _____

Pay to
the Order Of _____ $ _____

DOLLARS

LACY WEST
2299 FIRST STREET
PARK RIDGE, IL 60068
MEMO _____

1 1 2200 520 370 204 4323 111

Checks

Illinois Trust & Savings Bank
6193 Broadway
Park Ridge, IL 60068

1103
16-21/1222

_____ 19 _____

Pay to
The Order of _____ $ _____

_____ DOLLARS

LACY WEST
2299 FIRST STREET
PARK RIDGE, IL 60068

MEMO _____ _____

1122OO 52O 370 2O4 4223110

1. What is the name of the bank? _____

2. What is the number of the check? _____

3. Who can sign the check? _____

4. Where is the bank? _____

5. Write the check for $125.36. _____

6.. Make the check payable to State Co. Ins. _____

Checks

```
Illinois Trust & Savings Bank          1095
6193 Broadway                          16-21/1222
Park Ridge, IL 60068
                                  Aug. 22 19 95
PAY TO                                      $ 25.78
THE ORDER OF  Food Mart
Twenty-five + 78/100 ——————————— DOLLARS
LACY WEST
2299 FIRST STREET
PARK RIDGE, IL 60068
MEMO _____      Lacy West
112200 520 370 204 4323109
```

1. Who is the check from?_____

2. What is the number of the check? _____

3. Who is the check written to? _____

4. Where is the bank? _____

5. What's the date of the check? _____

6. How much is the check for?_____

```
Illinois Trust & Savings Bank          1118
6193 Broadway                          16-21/1222
Park Ridge, IL 60068
                                  _____ 19 _____
Pay to
the Order Of_____  $ _____
                                        DOLLARS
LACY WEST
2299 FIRST STREET
PARK RIDGE, IL 60068
MEMO_____  _____
112200 520 370 204 4323111
```

1. What is your classmate's name? _____

Write the name on the check.

2. Would he or she like some extra money? _____

3. How much would he or she like? _____

4. Write him or her a check. Be sure to fill out everything on the check.

A. When do you have to pay your rent?

B. I have to pay it on the first of the month.

A. When is the gas and electric bill due?

B. It's due on the 15th.

A. When do you have to pay your telephone bill?

B. It's due on the 30th.

Check what you have to pay each month.

_____	gas	_____	dentist
_____	electricity	_____	credit cards
_____	rent	_____	cable T.V.
_____	groceries	_____	savings
_____	telephone	_____	health insurance
_____	water	_____	school tuition
_____	car insurance	_____	child care
_____	car payment	_____	trash pick up
_____	clothes	_____	nursery school
_____	life insurance	_____	house payment
_____	doctor	_____	entertainment
		_____	donations to charity

Bob has many bills to pay in March.

			MARCH			
SUN.	MON.	TUE.	WED.	THU.	FRI.	SAT.
	1	2 WATER BILL DUE	3	4	5 CHILD CARE DUE	6
7	8 PAY DAY	9	10	11	12 CHILD CARE DUE	13
14	15 RENT DUE	16	17 PAY GAS AND ELECTRIC	18	19 CHILD CARE DUE	20
21	22 PAY DAY	23	24 CABLE DUE	25 PHONE BILL DUE	26 CHILD CARE DUE	27
28	29	30	31			

1. When is Bob's rent due? _____

2. When does Bob have to pay his water bill? _____

3. When does Bob pay his telephone bill?_____

4. When is the gas and electricity bill due? _____

5. When does Bob pay for child care? _____

6. When does Bob get paid? _____

7. When is the cable T.V. bill due? _____

Listen and fill in information about Sue's budget.

1. Sue's rent is _____ .

2. Sue's cable TV is _____ .

3. Sue's child care bill is _____ .

4. Sue's telephone bill is _____ .

5. Sue's gas and electric is _____ .

6. Sue's water bill is _____ .

7. How much money does Sue need to pay all these monthly bills?

   She needs _____ each month.

What about you?

1. My monthly rent is _____ .

2. My cable TV is_____ .

3. My child care bill is_____ .

4. My telephone bill is_____ .

5. My gas and electric is _____ .

6. My food costs about_____ .

7. My car payment is _____ .

8. My car insurance is_____ .

9. My _____ is _____ .

10. My _____ is _____ .

11. My _____ is _____ .

12. I need _____ a month.

A. What was your gas and electric bill last month?

B. It was $50, the same as usual.

A. Hmmm, mine was $90. It was higher than usual.

B. Call the company. Have them recheck your bill.

SAN DIEGO GAS & ELECTRIC CO.

ACCOUNT NUMBER	SERVICE ADDRESS	DATE PAST DUE
3697404351284	2984 FULTON ST.	06-05-94

TYPE OF SERVICE	METER READING		
	PRESENT	PREVIOUS	
	5/23	4/23	
GAS	560	390	20.37
ELECTRIC	3185	2980	25.37
AMOUNT DUE:			45.67

1. What's the account number? _____

2. When is this bill due?_____

3. What's the total amount due? _____

4. What's more expensive, gas or electricity?_____

5. Was more gas used this month or last? _____

A. I have a question about my bill.

B. What's your account number?

A. _____

B. Thank you. What's your question?

```
                                              PACIFIC [✱] TELL

RESIDENCE SERVICE FLAT RATE
ACCOUNT  NUMBER
619 555-1532 490 S 1164

                 STATEMENT DATE      MICHAEL W. WOO
                 NOV. 1 1994         8527 FRONT ST.
                                     SAN DIEGO, CA 92105

PREVIOUS    AMOUNT OF LAST BILL _____  58.66
CHARGES     PAYMENT. THANK YOU _____   58.66 CR
            BALANCE                             .00
CURRENT     PACIFIC BELL _____          20.56
CHARGES     LONG DISTANCE _____         56.91
            ZONE CALLS                          .60
TOTAL DUE   -DUE BY DEC. 1 1994                 78.07
-LATE CHARGE REMINDER : A LATE CHARGE MAY APPLY ON DEC. 3 IF
   YOUR PAYMENT HAS NOT BEEN RECEIVED. YOUR BILL, HOWEVER, MUST STILL
   BE PAID BEFORE THE "DUE BY" DATE TO AVOID ANY OTHER PENALTIES.
```

1. What's the account number? _____

2. How much was the bill last month? _____

3. How much was paid on last month's bill? _____

4. What month is this bill for?_____

5. How much is the long distance bill? _____

6. When is the bill due? _____

7. What are the current charges? _____

8. What's the name on the bill? _____

9. What's the total bill?_____

The Telephone Bill

```
┌─────────────────────────────────────────────────────────────┐
│ ▓▓▓▓▓▓▓▓▓▓▓▓▓▓▓▓▓▓▓▓▓▓▓▓▓▓▓▓▓▓▓        PACIFIC ✱ TELL        │
│                                                               │
│ RESIDENCE SERVICE FLAT RATE                                   │
│ ACCOUNT NUMBER                                                │
│ 619 555-1532 490 S 1164                                       │
│                                                               │
│            STATEMENT DATE        MICHAEL W. WOO               │
│             NOV. 1 1994          8527 FRONT ST.               │
│                                  SAN DIEGO, CA 92105          │
│                                                               │
│  PREVIOUS    AMOUNT OF LAST BILL _____  58.66      │
│  CHARGES     PAYMENT. THANK YOU  _____  58.66 CR   │
│              BALANCE                                .00       │
│  CURRENT     PACIFIC BELL                          20.56      │
│  CHARGES     LONG DISTANCE _____         56.91      │
│              ZONE CALLS                             .60       │
│  TOTAL DUE   — DUE BY DEC. 1 1994                  78.07      │
│                                                               │
│  —LATE CHARGE REMINDER : A LATE CHARGE MAY APPLY ON DEC. 3 IF │
│   YOUR PAYMENT HAS NOT BEEN RECEIVED. YOUR BILL, HOWEVER, MUST│
│   STILL BE PAID BEFORE THE "DUE BY" DATE TO AVOID ANY OTHER   │
│   PENALTIES.                                                  │
└─────────────────────────────────────────────────────────────┘
```

ZONE 1 CALLS

	DATE	TIME	PLACE & NUMBER CALLED		MINUTES	AMOUNT
1	NOV 10	5:18 PM	SAN DIEGO CA	619 299-2113	2	.10
2	NOV 16	10:13 PM	POWAY CA	619 528-7700	2	.10
3	NOV 21	11:22 AM	SAN DIEGO CA	619 222-8269	2	.06
4	NOV 23	12:48 PM	SAN DIEGO CA	619 582-7700	8	.15
5	NOV 24	4:59 PM	VISTA CA	619 528-8493	8	.15
6	NOV 30	12:34 PM	SAN DIEGO CA	619 582-7770	1	.04
				SUB-TOTAL		.60

Look at the telephone bill and answer the questions.

1. What's the account number? _____

2. What's the balance from the previous month? _____

3. How much is the call in item 1? _____

4. How much was the call on November 24? _____

5. What time was item 2 call made? _____

6. What time was item 4 call made? _____

7. Where was item 2 to? _____

8. How much was item 2? _____

9. How many minutes was item 3 call? _____

10. About how much a minute is that? _____

11. How many minutes was item 4 call? _____

12. About how much a minute is that? _____

13. What is the subtotal of zone calls? _____

14. What is the total due? _____

15. What long distance calls do you make? _____

Mailing Packages

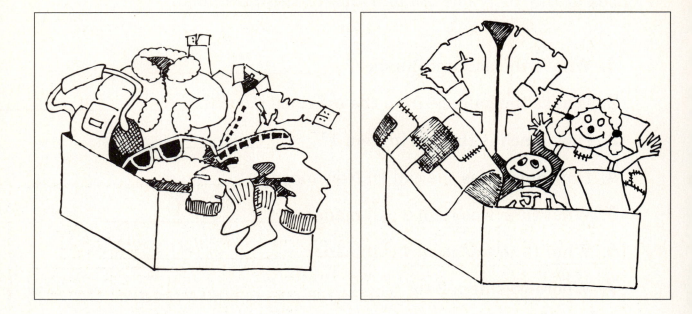

Package 1

What are the parcel contents?

1. _____

2. _____

3. _____

4. _____

What's the declared value of the parcel?

_____

Package 2

What are the parcel contents?

1. _____

2. _____

3. _____

4. _____

What's the declared value of the parcel?

_____

A. I would like to send this by UDS.

B. Fill out this form, please.

```
CUSTOMER    NAME _____        UNITED
SHIPPING    STREET _____   UDS  DELIVERY
RECORD:     CITY _____         SERVICE

COMPLETE ALL INFORMATION BELOW        FOR UPS USE ONLY
   NAME _____
   STREET _____
1  CITY _____ STATE ____ ZIP ____
   PACKAGE CONTENTS:

   NAME _____
   STREET _____
2  CITY _____ STATE ____ ZIP ____
   PACKAGE CONTENTS:

   NAME _____
   STREET _____
3  CITY _____ STATE ____ ZIP ____
   PACKAGE CONTENTS:

   NAME _____
   STREET _____
4  CITY _____ STATE ____ ZIP ____       THANK YOU FOR
   PACKAGE CONTENTS:                          USING — U D S
```

Yes or No

Ask your classmate the question. Check if the answer is **Yes**; leave blank if the answer is **No**.

Have you paid the _____ bill this month?

_____ **1.** gas

_____ **2.** rent

_____ **3.** newspaper

_____ **4.** telephone

_____ **5.** water

_____ **6.** car insurance

_____ **7.** credit card

_____ **8.** cable TV

_____ **9.** life insurance

_____ **10.** electricity

_____ **11.** school tuition

_____ **12.** child care

_____ **13.** trash pick–up

_____ **14.** pre-school

_____ **15.** car

_____ **16.** dentist

_____ **17.** doctor

Appliance Store Window

A. Can I help you?

B. Yes, I'm interested in a refrigerator.

A. We have a wonderful model here. It's 22 cubic feet.

B. That's larger than I need.

A. We have this beautiful side-by-side. It's 21 cubic feet and has an ice-maker, and it's very energy efficient.

B. Oh, no. I'm looking for a basic model with a freezer.

A. Here it is. Your basic, 17 cubic foot, white refrigerator. It's also an energy efficient model.

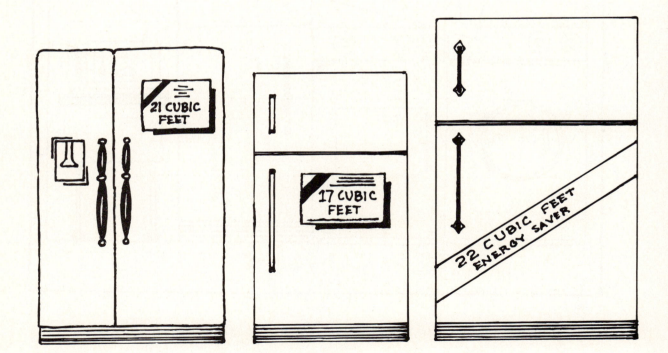

Words That Describe

Put the words in order to describe the underlined item. The first one is done for you.

1. refrigerator, large, yellow, frostless

large, yellow frostless refrigerator

2. 500-watt, portable, microwave white

_____

3. 3-temperature, washer, 2-water level, heavy-duty

_____

4. 4-track, remote control, VCR, quality

_____

5. dependable, 2-temperature, extra large, dryer, push-button

_____

6. steam iron, 7-temperature, automatic off

_____

7. stereo, excellent, top-of-the-line

_____

8. Describe your TV. _____

_____

9. Describe your radio. _____

_____

10. Describe last weekend. _____

A. Are you interested in a washing machine?

B. Yes, I am. I want to see the one advertised in the paper.

A. Here it is. It's $550.

B. Is there a warranty?

A. Yes, for one year.

B. Is there a delivery charge?

A. Yes, it's $20.

B. Is there an installation charge?

A. Yes, it's $30. We also have a low-interest, easy-payment credit plan.

FULL ONE-YEAR WARRANTY

WE WARRANT THIS PRODUCT TO BE FREE OF PROBLEMS FOR 1 YEAR AFTER THE DATE OF PURCHASE. THIS WARRANTY DOES NOT INCLUDE DAMAGE TO THE PRODUCT FROM ACCIDENT, IMPROPER INSTALLATION OR UNAUTHORIZED REPAIR. IF THE PRODUCT SHOULD BREAK WITHIN THE WARRANTY PERIOD WE WILL REPLACE IT FREE OF CHARGE. FOR INSTRUCTIONS ON HOW TO OBTAIN WARRANTY SERVICE WRITE TO: G.E. CONSUMER ELECTRONICS PRODUCTS, CONSUMER RELATIONS, P.O. BOX 1976 INDIANAPOLIS, INDIANA 46206

What do you think?

1. How long is the warranty good for? _____

2. Do you need to mail in a card to register the warranty? _____

3. Do you need your cash receipt? _____

4. What does the warranty cover? _____

5. Where do you take the product for repair while it is under warranty?

_____

Charges

Item	Price	Warranty	Delivery Charge	Installation Charge
Washer	$425.00	1year	$20.00	$30.00
Refrigerator	$575.00	6 months	$25.00	0
Microwave	$280.00	30 days	n/a	n/a
Video Cassette Recorder	$319.00	30 days	n/a	n/a

1. How much does the refrigerator cost? _____

2. Is there a delivery charge? _____

3. Is there an installation charge? _____

4. How much does the microwave cost? _____

5. Does it have a warranty? _____

Rosa's Problem

Rosa has a difficult problem. Let's help. Rosa is a single parent. She is raising four children, ages 10, 12, 14, and 16. She works part time so she can be with her children as much as possible.

Of course Rosa loves them all very much. They all go to school, and they are earning good grades. They are nice kids. They help around the house and care for each other. Rosa's 16 year old son wants a new stereo.

The stereo he wants costs $375. Rosa doesn't have enough money for the stereo and groceries. She thinks the stereo is important to her son, and she wants him to be happy. What can she do?

Here are five words from the story. Underline them in the story. Use each in a sentence.

1. raising _____

2. possible _____

3. earning _____

4. care for _____

5. enough _____

Rosa's Story

Answer these questions about Rosa's story.

1. Who is this story about? _____

2. What is the problem? _____

_____

3. When did this story happen? _____

4. Where did this story happen? _____

_____

Talk About It:

1. Rosa can get another part-time job.

2. The son can get a part-time job.

3. They can borrow the money from a relative.

4. She can take the money from her savings because the son is a good boy.

5. They can wait for a holiday and buy the stereo for a gift.

6. Do you have a different solution? _____

_____

_____

7. What solution do you think is best? _____

_____

_____

8. Why do you think this is the best solution? _____

_____

8

TRAVELING

A. Where would you like to go on vacation?

B. I'd like to go | gambling in Las Vegas.
camping in the mountains.
shopping downtown.
sightseeing in Washington, D.C.

Would you like to go, too?

A. Sure. Sometime I would.

I	would wouldn't	like to go	gambling fishing camping hiking shopping sightseeing driving dancing	in a night club. downtown. in the mountains. in the country. in Miami. in Las Vegas. at the beach. in the mall. in the desert.

Use the chart above. Write five true sentences about yourself.

1. _____
_____

2. _____
_____

3. _____
_____

4. _____
_____

5. _____
_____

Equipment

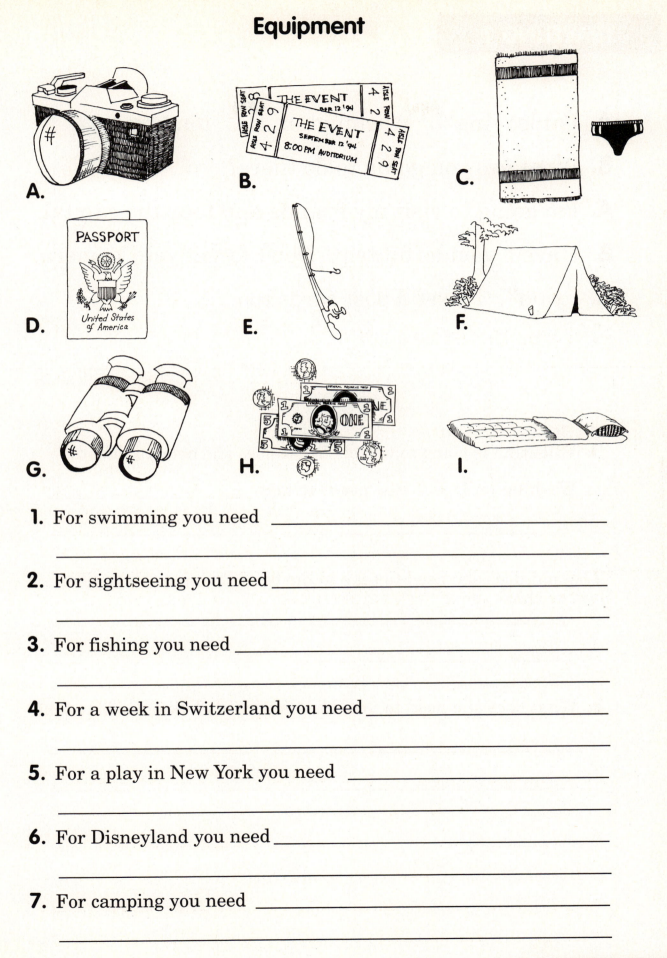

A.

B.

C.

D.

E.

F.

G.

H.

I.

1. For swimming you need _____

_____

2. For sightseeing you need _____

_____

3. For fishing you need _____

_____

4. For a week in Switzerland you need _____

_____

5. For a play in New York you need _____

_____

6. For Disneyland you need _____

_____

7. For camping you need _____

_____

A. I'm leaving for Washington, D.C. tomorrow.

B. What are you going to do there?

A. I'm going to visit my friends and tour the capital.

B. Have a wonderful trip. Don't forget your camera.

A. I won't. I'll send post cards too.

1. Valentina is going to travel. What does she need to take to Washington D. C.? She needs to take _____

_____

2. What does she need to take to the beach? She needs to take

_____

_____

3. What does she need to take to Atlantic City? She needs to take

_____

_____

A. I can't find my camera anywhere.

B. Where have you looked?

A. I've looked in my room. I've looked in my bag.

B. Have you looked around your neck?

A. Oops! Thanks.

Have you looked...

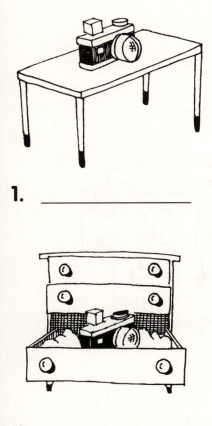

1. _____

2. _____

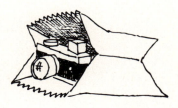

3. _____

4. _____

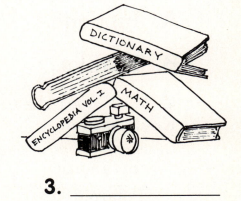

5. _____

Where is your camera?

6. _____

A. I need some film.

B. What kind?

A. 35 mm.

B. Do you want a roll of 36 exposures or 24 exposures?

A. 36.

B. Color?

A. Yes.

B. How many rolls do you want?

A. Just one.

B. Thanks.

Kinds of film:

instamatic
Polaroid
video
35 mm slide
35 mm print
110
disc

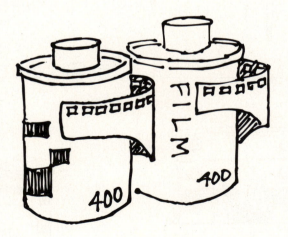

Postcards

Dear Friends,
Having a great time in Washington D.C. I want to see the White House, the Capitol Building, and the Lincoln Memorial. Would you like a souvenir? I'm going to England next. You can write me at

29 The Frogmarket
Worcester, WR11DD
England
Valentina

English Second Language Class
2204 Comstock St.
San Diego, CA
92111

Write a postcard to Valentina.

Postcards

Dear Friends,
I arrived in London last night. It was cold and damp. How's the weather there? Today I'm going sightseeing in London. Maybe I'll see the Queen. I would like to see the Prime Minister also. I can't remember his name. Please write me at the same address.

Valentina

English Second Language Class
2204 Comstock St.
San Diego, CA 92111

Write Valentina another card.

A. Can I help you?

B. Yes, I want to mail these postcards to England. How much is a stamp?

A. It's _____.

B. Thanks, I'll take five stamps.

****

A. Can I help you?

B. I want to mail this letter to _____. How much is a stamp?

A. It's _____.

B. How long does it take to get there?

A. It will get there in _____ days.

B. Thanks.

I want to mail this _____.

How much is the | stamp?
| postage?

  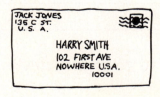 

1. _____ **2.** _____ **3.** _____

A Letter from Valentina

Dear Friends,
    Thank you for your postcard. It's nice to have friends. I love London. What a busy city! It's very old. Some streets are narrow. It's cool here. Every day we walk around to see the old churches, parliament buildings and shops. At 4:00 we drink tea.
    Tomorrow I'm going to Berlin, Germany to see my cousins. I'll be there three days. I'm going to the museums. Then I'm going to Moscow to see my mother. I'm very excited. Please write me at
      Puszczyka 4.44
      02-777 Moscow
      Russia   *Valentina*

Answer the questions.

1. Where is Valentina now? _____

2. Where is she going tomorrow? _____

3. How long will she be there? _____

4. What will she see in Berlin? _____

    _____

    _____

5. Why is she excited to go to Moscow? _____

    _____

    _____

Write a letter to Valentina.

1. Write the date.

2. Write the greeting: Dear or Hello.

3. Write the letter. Ask Valentina some questions, and tell her about yourself.

4. Write a closing: Love or Sincerely.

5. Don't forget to sign your name.

Another Letter from Valentina

Dear Friends,

How are you? I'm fine and really happy to see my mother and many old friends.

Moscow is a large city full of government officials and businessmen. It's a very exciting place. St. Basil's Cathedral is beautiful. Today we're going to see the Kremlin. I'd like to tell the President how much we all want peace.

Well, I hope your school year is fine.

Good-bye for now,

Valentina

Answer the questions.

1. Who is Valentina visiting in Moscow? _____

2. What can you see in Moscow? _____

_____

3. What do we all want, everywhere, and for everyone?

_____

A. Have you heard from Valentina?

B. She called me last night.

A. Really? What did she say?

B. She told me to tell you that she's going to Egypt.

A. How wonderful! What's she going to do there?

B. She told me not to tell you, but she's getting married!

Retrace Valentina's trip with your pencil.

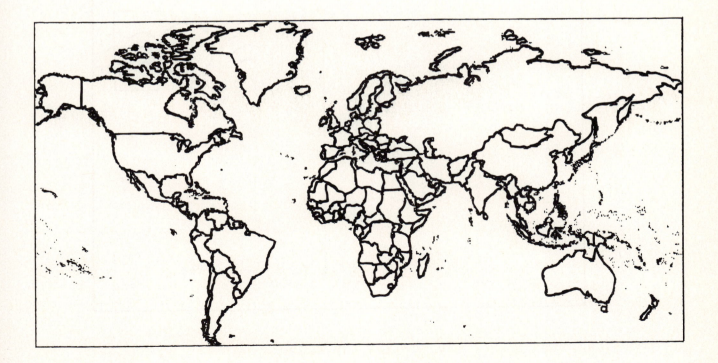

Postcards

Dear Friends,
I'm very happy to tell you my good news. I met an old friend in Moscow. We just got married! We're visiting his parents in Cairo, Egypt now. Egypt is a very romantic place. I love the pyramids.

Valentina

English Second Language Class
2204 Comstock St.
San Diego, CA
92111

Send your best wishes to Valentina.

Where has Valentina been? Review her postcards to fill in the chart.

	country	capitol city	title of leader	name of leader	famous sights
first	**United States**				
second					
third					
fourth					
fifth					

Answer the questions.

1. Where has Valentina been? _____

_____

2. Where did she go first? _____

3. Who is the leader of the United States?

_____

4. What did Valentina do in Washington, D.C.? _____

_____

5. Where did she go after Washington, D.C.? _____

6. What is the capital of Great Britain? _____

7. What country did Valentina visit next? _____

8. Who is the leader of Germany? _____

9. What is the capital of Russia.? _____

10. Who is the leader of Russia? _____

11. Where did Valentina visit after Russia? _____

12. What's the capital of Egypt? _____

13. What did Valentina see in Moscow? _____

_____

14. What did she do in Cairo? _____

_____

A. Can you help me fill out this envelope?

B. Sure. What kind of film did you use?

A. 35 mm.

B. Do you want 3 inch pictures or larger 4 inch ones?

A. 4 inch ones.

B. How many pictures did you take?

A. 24.

B. O.K. Now, just fill out the top.

A. Thanks.

A. I can't find my film.

B. Did you look in the | file? |
                            | bin? |

A. Yes, I did, but it's not there. Could you check behind the desk?

B. O.K. What's the last name?

A. Ban.

B. Van?

A. No, **B** as in a-**B**-c. B-a-n.

B. O.K. Do you have the | claim slip? |
                              | receipt? |

A. Here. Thanks for checking.

Fill in the missing letter.

1. a ____ c	7. l ____ n	13. x ____ z
2. o ____ q	8. c ____ e	14. k ____ m
3. v ____ x	9. d ____ f	15. e ____ g
4. f ____ h	10. h ____ j	16. i ____ k
5. r ____ t	11. s ____ u	17. n ____ p
6. d ____ f	12. b ____ d	18. g ____ i

M FIRST LETTER OF LAST NAME 438 624141

ONE ROLL OF FILM PER ENVELOPE

PLEASE PRINT
LAST NAME Maltz FIRST Howard

ADDRESS

CITY   STATE   ZIP

FILM TYPE
☒ COLOR
☐ SLIDES OR MOVIE
☐ BLACK & WHITE
☐ OTHER

FILM SIZE   NO. OF EXP.
☐ 35mm ☐ 12
☐ DISC   ☐ 15
☐ 110   ☒ 24
☒ 126   ☐ 36

CHECK HERE FOR:
☐ REPRINTS
☐ 5 × 7
☐ 8 × 10
☐ OTHER

YOUR CHOICE

3" PRINTS ☐ CHECK HERE

4" PRINTS ☒ CHECK HERE

SPECIAL INSTRUCTIONS:

CHECK HERE FOR MATTE FINISH _ _ _ ☐

Bobbie Cee's PHOTO SERVICE

PRICE 4.58

Answer the questions.

1. How much are the pictures? _____

2. Whose film is this? _____

3. Did the person remember his address? _____

4. Did the person use 126 film?_____

5. Did the person remember to fill in the first initial of the last name?

   _____

6. Did the person want 3 inch prints or 4 inch prints? _____

7. Did the person have special instructions? _____

8. Have you had film developed? _____

Capital Letters

The names of people, countries, states, and places begin with capital letters. The first letter of an abbreviation is also capitalized.

Find the words in the sentences below that should have capital letters. Correct them.

1. valentina has been in the united states, great britain, germany, egypt, and russia.

2. washington, d.c., is the capital of the united states.

3. In russia there are many mosques.

4. moscow is the capital city of russia.

5. The president of russia and the president of the united states both want world peace.

6. berlin is the capitol of germany.

7. chancellor _____ is the leader of germany.

8. valentina is russian, and her husband is egyptian, but they will live in the united states.

9

SPECIAL DAYS

A. What's your favorite day?

B. It's Friday because | it's the end of the week.
it's the start of the week-end. |

What's yours?

A. It's | payday.
my birthday.
Christmas.
New Year's.
my anniversary.
Thanksgiving.
_____ . |

B. Oh, why?

A. Because _____ .

Interview three people. Ask what their favorite day is and why.

Name	Favorite day	Why
1.		
2.		
3.		

A. It's my friend's birthday, and I want to buy him a present.

B. What are you going to get him?

A. I don't know. He likes music.

B. You could get him a cassette tape.

Suggest some presents. Use him or her.

1. She likes to garden. You could buy _____.

2. He likes cars. You could get _____.

3. My aunt likes to read. _____.

4. His uncle likes movies. _____.

5. My mother likes to exercise. _____.

6. My father likes to cook. _____.

7. My sister likes photography. _____.

8. Grandfather likes baseball. _____.

9. Grandmother likes to fish. _____.

10. Nu likes to collect stamps. _____.

11. Jose likes to dance. _____.

12. I like to _____. _____.

Superstitions

What is a superstition? Do you have a lucky number? Some people think that Friday the thirteenth is a very unlucky day. They're afraid they'll have an accident or lose something. Some people stay home on Friday the thirteenth because they're afraid of having bad luck. People believe this, but it isn't true. This is called a superstition.

Usually we enjoy superstitions because we have fun with them. There are many superstitions. Here are some. You'll have bad luck if a black cat walks in front of you, if you break a mirror, or if you walk under a ladder. You'll have good luck if you find a penny, if you catch the bride's bouquet at a wedding, or if you find a four-leaf clover.

Some people are very superstitious and think that all superstitions are true. No one knows where or how superstitions start.

Talk about it.

1. Is the number thirteen unlucky in your country?

2. Do you have a lucky number?

3. Do you have an unlucky number?

4. Tell a superstition you know.

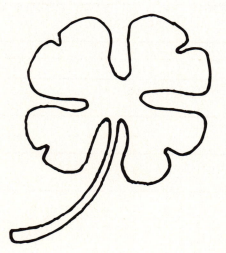

Good Luck - Bad Luck

1. Have you had bad luck? _____

2. What bad luck have you had? _____

   _____

3. Have you had good luck? _____

4. What good luck have you had? _____

5. A lucky person has good luck. An unlucky person has bad luck.

   Are you lucky or unlucky? _____

6. Do you know a lucky person? _____

7. Why is he or she lucky? _____

8. Do you know an unlucky person? _____

9. Why is he or she unlucky? _____

10. Some people say that finding a four-leaf clover brings good luck and
    that walking under a ladder brings bad luck. In your native country,
    what brings you good luck?

    _____

11. In your native country, what brings you bad luck?

    _____

12. Share your answers with your neighbor.

The New Year

In the United States we celebrate New Year's Eve on December thirty-first and New Year's Day on January first. People go to parties on New Year's Eve. They stay up all night singing and dancing. They see the old year out and the new year in. At midnight on New Year's Eve, everyone wishes a happy New Year to family and friends.

The next day, January first, is New Year's Day. It's the first day of the calendar year.

For all people the new year is an opportunity to change old habits or begin something new. Some people try to stop smoking, return to school, learn to drive, or improve their diet. These are called resolutions.

Match the two columns.

_____ 1. midnight   a. hopes for

_____ 2. resolution   b. chance or time

_____ 3. wishes   c. behaviors

_____ 4. calendar year   d. enjoy and party

_____ 5. opportunity   e. 12:00 PM

_____ 6. habits   f. night before

_____ 7. celebrate   g. January 1 to December 31

_____ 8. eve   h. promise

Abraham Lincoln

Abraham Lincoln was our sixteenth president. He is well known, but his private life was tragic.

Lincoln was born February 12, 1809. He started working in politics in his early twenties. He was elected president when he was 51. While he was president, the southern states tried to separate from the northern states. Then the Civil War began. When the war ended, the southern states remained a part of the United States, and the slaves were free people.

Lincoln married Mary Todd in 1842. She was from a wealthy family but Lincoln's family was poor. Mary was short and plump. Lincoln was tall and thin. They had four sons.

They were a very busy and happy family. Then tragedy came into their family. One son died, and the Lincolns became very depressed. Then another son died and Mary seemed to go crazy. She began "seeing" her two dead sons every night. Mary wanted Lincoln to go to seances in the White House.

In 1865, when Lincoln was 56 years old, he was assassinated by John Wilkes Booth. Some people say Abraham Lincoln's ghost still lives in the White House. Lincoln does live on in our hearts for freeing the slaves and for keeping our country together.

Here are five words from the story. Underline them in the story. Use each in a new sentence.

1. private _____

2. tragic_____

3. politics _____

4. slaves _____

5. separate _____

Abe Lincoln

Circle correct answer.

1. Abe Lincoln was the 16th President of the U.S.   Yes   No

2. He married Mary Todd, who was rich, plump, and a little strange.   Yes   No

3. Two of Lincoln's sons died young.   Yes   No

4. He had two daughters who lived.   Yes   No

5. Lincoln and his wife really loved their family.   Yes   No

6. Mary Lincoln was depressed because her two sons died.   Yes   No

7. Lincoln was president before he was 43.   Yes   No

8. Mary wanted to go to seances to talk to her dead children.   Yes   No

9. The Lincolns lived in the White House before he became president.   Yes   No

10. Lincoln died of old age.   Yes   No

11. Some people say they can see Lincoln's ghost in the White House.   Yes   No

12. Lincoln freed the slaves.   Yes   No

13. Lincoln did not let the North and South separate.   Yes   No

George Washington

Did you know that George Washington had wooden false teeth? That's not very romantic. George Washington was born February 22, 1732. He died December 14, 1799. He was 67. George worked hard on his family's farm. His father died when he was eleven.

George wanted to run away to sea, but his mother wouldn't let him. When George was seventeen he worked as a surveyor. He never attended college.

Washington was a romantic young man. He loved to dance and flirt with ladies. He fell in love with a married woman, but he never married her. She was very thin and beautiful, and two years older than Washington.

Washington married a short, plump, and friendly woman named Martha. She was a very rich widow with two children. Over the years George and Martha became very close. Martha was a homebody and liked to cook. They never had children of their own.

Washington was a strong leader. He kept the thirteen colonies together for the birth of our country. The people elected George Washington the first president of the new United States in 1789.

Here are five words from the story. Underline them in the story. Use them in the story.

1. attended _____

2. romantic _____

3. flirt _____

4. homebody _____

5. leader _____

Reread the story and complete these sentences.

1. Washington _____ _____ February 22, 1732
   and _____ December 14, 1799.

2. George wanted _____ _____ _____ _____
   _____, but his mother wouldn't let him.

3. George worked as a _____.

4. He _____ _____ to college.

5. Washington was a _____ young man.

6. He loved to _____ and _____ _____ ladies.

7. Washington _____ _____ _____ with a married
   woman.

8. The married woman was thin and _____.

9. He married a _____ widow with two
   _____.

10. Martha was a _____. She liked to
    _____.

11. Washington was a _____ leader.

12. He kept the colonies together for the _____.

13. He was the _____ president of the United States.

George Washington

1. What did George want to do to when he was young?

_____

2. When did his father die? _____

3. How old was Washington when he started working

as a surveyor?

_____

4. Where did he go to college? _____

5. Who did George Washington fall in love with?

_____

6. Who did he marry? _____

7. How many children did he have? _____

8. How old was Washington when he died? _____

9. Which president was he? _____

10. What kind of man was he? _____

_____

11. Why do we remember George Washington?

_____

_____

The Fourth of July

The Fourth of July is the birthday of the United States. It's a national holiday. It was the day we declared our independence from England. On July 4, 1776, 56 men from the thirteen colonies signed the declaration paper.

Today, Americans celebrate in many ways. They have picnics and barbecues. They watch parades. They visit parks and beaches and watch the fireworks. Fireworks are illegal in many areas of our country. That means individuals can't use or buy them. People enjoy the professional firework shows. The shows are spectacular every Fourth of July. Everyone loves the fireworks.

Here are five words from the story. Underline them in the story. Use each in new sentence.

1. declared _____

2. independence _____

3. celebrate _____

4. illegal _____

5. spectacular _____

List some of the native countries of students in your classroom. What day does each country celebrate its independence? What country is each independent of?

Country	Date of holiday	Separated from what country?
1. _____		
2. _____		
3. _____		
4.		

1. What's the birthday of the United States? _____

2. What country used to rule the United States? _____

3. What's the birthday of your native country? _____

4. How is it celebrated?

_____

5. Did you watch fireworks in your native country? _____

6. What holiday or holidays are celebrated with fireworks in your native country?

_____

_____

_____

The Declaration of Independence
July 4, 1776

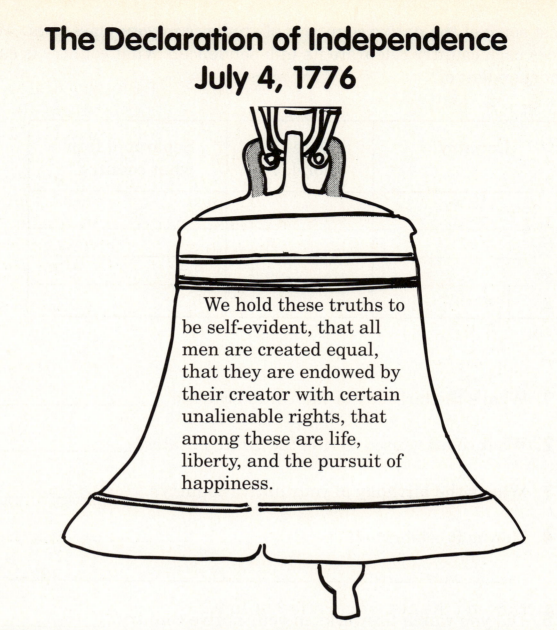

We hold these truths to be self-evident, that all men are created equal, that they are endowed by their creator with certain unalienable rights, that among these are life, liberty, and the pursuit of happiness.

Fifty-six men signed the Declaration of Independence. After the men signed it, they rang the Liberty Bell. The Liberty Bell is a symbol of our freedom. The Declaration of Independence said that the thirteen colonies were free and independent from England. England said the people who signed the declaration were traitors.

A war began between the colonies and England. England lost. The thirteen colonies became the United States.

1. _____ lost the war for independence.

2. _____ won the Revolutionary War.

3. In the United States all men _____,
and we have unalienable _____.

The First Day of School

I remember my first day of school in the U.S. I started school on September 14, 1988. My first teacher was Mrs. Paul.

I couldn't speak English. I told my teacher, "I want to move to a lower class." My teacher said there wasn't a lower class. She told me to try for two weeks.

I remember I was always nervous, but sometimes I was happy. After two weeks I was usually happy.

I decided school was fun.

1. Who was the teacher? _____

2. What was the problem at first? _____

_____

3. How did the new student feel at first?

_____

4. How did the new student feel later? _____

_____

5. What is the story about? _____

_____

_____

I Remember My First Day of School

Talk about it. Then, write about it.

1. Do you remember your first day of school in the United States?

_____

_____

2. Where did you go to school?_____

3. Did you feel nervous? _____

4. Did you feel shy?_____

5. Did you go to school with somebody you knew? _____

6. Did you feel afraid? _____

7. What was your teacher's name? _____

8. What do you remember about the first day of school?

_____

_____

_____

9. What's different about schools in the U.S. and schools in your native country?

_____

_____

_____

_____

_____

_____

10. What's the same about the schools?

_____

_____

_____

Thanksgiving

Thanksgiving is on the fourth Thursday of November. On this day we give thanks for all the wonderful things we have.

The Pilgrims came to the New World from England in the winter of 1620. They wanted religious freedom.

The Pilgrims didn't know how to grow food to survive in this new land. The Indians showed the Pilgrims how to farm and what crops to plant. The Indians helped the Pilgrims.

One year later, in 1621, the Pilgrims celebrated. They celebrated because they were thankful. They prepared a feast of turkey, corn, squash, and cranberries. The Pilgrims invited the Indians to eat with them. The Pilgrims and the Indians shared a wonderful meal.

The Pilgrims gave thanks for their religious freedom in the new land. They gave thanks for their families. They gave thanks for their friends. They gave thanks for their food.

We continue to celebrate Thanksgiving by eating many of the same foods. We too are thankful for important things in our lives.

1. The first Pilgrims came from _____ in _____.

2. I came from _____ in _____ .

3. The _____ helped the Pilgrims.

4. _____ helped me.

5. The Pilgrims gave thanks for _____

_____

A Thanksgiving Poem

We, the students in this class are thankful for:

1. _____
2. _____
3. _____
4. _____
5. _____
6. _____
7. _____
8. _____
9. _____
10. _____
11. _____
12. _____
13. _____
14. _____
15. _____
16. _____
17. _____
18. _____
19. _____
20. _____
21. _____
22. _____
23. _____
24. _____

Check the places that are closed on these holidays.

Holidays for the year	Date	Post Offices	Libraries	Schools	Stores	Banks
New Years Day	Jan. 1					
Martin Luther King's Birthday	Jan. 16					
Lincoln's Birthday	Feb. 12					
Valentine's Day	Feb. 14					
Washington's Birthday	Feb. 22					
Easter						
Memorial Day	May 30					
Independence Day	Jul. 4					
Labor Day	1st Mon. in Sept.					
Halloween	Oct. 31					
Veteran's Day	Nov. 11					
Thanksgiving	4th Thur. in Nov.					
Christmas	Dec. 25					
New Year's Day	Dec. 31					

Holidays

Talk about it. Then, write about it.

1. Do you enjoy American holidays? _____

   _____

2. What is your favorite American holiday?

   _____

3. What is the biggest holiday in your native country?

   _____

4. When is the holiday?_____

5. Is this a religious holiday? _____
   Do you do special things? _____
   What activities do you do? _____

   _____

6. Do you wear special clothes? _____
   What clothes do you wear? _____

   _____

   _____

7. Do you eat special foods? _____ What are they?

   _____

8. Do you decorate your house? _____ How do you decorate?

   _____

9. What holidays are celebrated in your native country that are
   also celebrated in the United States?

   _____